SUNNY JIM

The Life of America's
Most Beloved Horseman—
James Fitzsimmons

Jimmy Breslin

ILLUSTRATED WITH PHOTOGRAPHS

Doubleday & Company, Inc.
Garden City, New York
1962

Contents

List of Illustrations

SUNNY JIM

1. Life Begins at Seventy-Seven

At about seven o'clock, when the dusk had changed the color of the hills and lake to gray flannel, the mosquitoes at Fitzsimmonsville, New York, which is a summer colony outside of Saratoga Springs, began to come out and eat Irish for dinner. Somebody turned on an automatic spraying system which pumps an insecticide smoke out of pipes on each of the six houses. When it began, everybody started to tell the great-grandfather, Mr. James E. Fitzsimmons, age eighty-seven, that he'd better walk down the hill to the lake so that the fumes wouldn't get a chance to clog his windpipe, which even he concedes is just a little bit odd.

It was nothing more than an extra precaution. The smoke had no smell to it at all; two martinis on somebody's breath would have been far more powerful. But the old man still made his way down the hill, a handkerchief in his hand to cover the outside chance this smoke business one of the family's engineers had devised would start him coughing.

One of the children playing on the hill saw him walking away. She promptly put a hand over her mouth, made herself cough and then flew down the hill. The one playing with her did the same and so did the others and now the hill was a tangle of barefeet in T-shirts and all of them had a hand over the mouth and kept forcing coughs.

"They see me," the old man said, "and they all start coughing. They didn't even know the spray was on. They just like to do it because I do it."

There were probably twenty-five kids running from the smoke. It was impossible to get an actual count because they moved around so fast.

"Do you know them all by name?" the old man was asked.

"Oh, this isn't even all of them," he said. "There's more around someplace. I guess I could try to pick them out here for you, but I stopped doin' that a long time ago. I always get them mixed up and then the mothers start squawking because I don't know their children. So I just say hello and pat them on the head."

The old man got down to the edge of the lake and stood there as the children ran around him. A group of older ones came down and got into the two motorboats which were tied to the dock. Up in one of the houses on the hill, the teen-age girls were in the kitchen, running up a phone bill with long-distance calls to a disk jockey in Albany who announces your name when he plays a request. There were also something like twenty-two adults getting dressed for a formal dinner. And three or four others, including the old man, were going to stay behind and baby-sit.

Earlier in the day, most of them had gone to the railroad station to say hello to granddaughter Eadith, who is a Sister of St. Joseph and was passing through on the afternoon train to Plattsburgh.

So many of the family had clustered on the platform in front of the one car that the old New York Central conductor said to a trainman with him, "I guess it's some sort of a celebrity they're here for. I'll take a walk down and make sure everything's all right. Maybe we can give 'em an extra minute for autographs and make it up somewhere along the line."

"It's no celebrity," a fellow working at the station told him. "It's a nun. Her family came to see her."

The conductor walked down to the car and held the train until everybody had a chance to say goodbye to Sister Anella, as she now is called.

"That's some family you've got," he said to one of the girls on the platform.

"Oh, we have a lot more than this," she told him.

Which they certainly do. There are, simply, an awful lot of Fitzsimmonses. And next year, Irish Roman Catholic couples being as they are, there will be even more of them.

And now, the old man who started the whole thing off, was standing by the lake and talking about how he was going to baby-sit later on.

"I'm the back-up man," he said. "Something happens to Eddie up there, I take over. Oh, I'll know what to do. I remember there was a fella back in Brooklyn, Brennan his name was, he was a corker at it. He used to get the kids, he had six of 'em, and he'd sit them in a circle around a big potbellied stove in the living room. Then he'd open up a bottle of beer and pass it around to them. He'd come back a half hour later and all he'd have to do is reach down, pick them up and carry them in to bed. They'd all be out like lights on the floor."

He stood there and watched the water and talked about baby-sitting until the insect smoke was turned off and he could go back up to one of the houses and sit down.

This is as good a place as any to begin picking up the story of James E. Fitzsimmons. He is a trainer of race horses who is called Sunny Jim Fitzsimmons in the newspapers, but Mr. Fitz by those who know him, and he is one of the biggest successes the sports world has ever had. He has been in horse racing since he was eleven and he has been a part of some days in sports history that most people, even if they have never seen a horse race, know something about. But the story of Mr. Fitz really isn't about horse racing. If it were, we would get down to bedrock right about here and go into such matters

13

as three-horse parlays and a bibliography of reasonable ex-
cuses for any milkman with a bill. The horse racing is just a
backdrop here because this is about a unique human being
who even now, at eighty-seven, is up at five in the morning,
six days a week, to start another day in the game of life that
he has beaten in a way that few ever have.

There are a lot of things about Mr. Fitz. He is old and bent
over, but he is active and smart and talented and his thinking
consists of today and tomorrow and next week and never yesterday. He is a great success at his business, but he is an even
bigger winner as a human being, which is something you do
not find often. Too many times, when you start telling about
somebody who is revered and has made it big, his wife or
his children come around and they tell you enough to make
you drop the whole project.

Mr. Fitz has been around for a long time: Sheepshead Bay
in the 1880s, Churchill Downs in the 1930s, or Belmont Park
and Aqueduct in 1961. But if you were to stand at a bar and
spend an afternoon talking to people about him, you would
have to start by saying that for the Sunny Jim Fitzsimmons
who is around today, a new life began at seventy-seven.

It started about 1946 when Mrs. James E. Fitzsimmons, sitting at home in Sheepshead Bay, Brooklyn, decided to get a
little puckish about life. She made up her mind that she was
old and she would like a little service. For sixty-one years of
her married life she had done everything from selling the
living-room furniture to having children practically unaided.
Now that her husband had become a famous sports figure—or
at least the newspapers said he was famous—and the children
were married, she thought it was about time somebody made
a fuss over her.

First there were the newspapers. Jennie Fitzsimmons had
been a front-page to back-page reader of newspapers all her
life, but now she would sit in the living room and hold the
paper close to her face and then throw it down and tell every-

body, "I'm getting too old to read. I can't see the print any more. I'm just too old."

Then there was her Holy Communion on the first Friday of the month. Mrs. Fitzsimmons always went to Mass on these Fridays and received Communion, in addition to Sundays and Holy Days. During all her years in Sheepshead Bay, she would make it to St. Mark's, five blocks away, through any sort of weather. There were certain things in life you could count on and one of them was Mrs. Fitzsimmons making it to St. Mark's. But now it was different. She informed Father Edward Lahey that she was just too old and too tired to make it down to St. Mark's on first Fridays and would he please come to her house and give Communion, as parish priests do for all who are physically unable to come out. Of course, Father Lahey said he'd be around.

There were other things like this. And when they were put together they would have worried those around her, except for certain things that happened. One Friday, for example, her family noticed that Mrs. Fitz, who had been sitting in the living room downstairs, jumped up and ran to her bedroom as Father Lahey came up the front walk to give Communion to his shut-in. After this, the family clocked her in track record time for the distance on several of these sprints.

Grandson Jimmy also became a bit skeptical during one of his weekly drives with her. Every Thursday afternoon, from the time Jimmy was old enough to drive, he and his grandmother got in the car and went someplace—upstate New York, out on Long Island; anyplace they felt like. They'd eat dinner, then come home. On one of these drives, following a round of complaints about her eyes and general failing health, Mrs. Fitzsimmons was sitting next to Jimmy as they were driving through upstate on the way back to Brooklyn.

A good distance away, far enough to make an eye doctor squint, a stately house sat on the top of one of those rolling hills which edge out from either bank of the Hudson River.

15

"That's a pretty house," Jimmy said. "Must be a beautiful view from inside it."

"Oh yes, it is," his grandmother agreed. "And they have a lovely window arrangement. See it? Four right in a row across the top and then two together on each side of the door. They must have a lovely view from the living room and top bedroom."

Her grandson could not make out the windows if his life hinged on it. Neither could nine out of ten people. So her old age and infirmities turned into one of those little games people always like to play with one another and nobody had much to worry about.

By the spring of 1951, Sunny Jim Fitzsimmons was approaching his seventy-seventh birthday and people were calling him ancient. He had lived a full life, and now it was becoming serene. He was at the barn each morning with the hay and ammonia smell opening his eyes and flaring his nostrils as it always had, and then he would train his horses, have something to eat, take a nap and wake up for the afternoon's racing. There was almost no change. You could spend a day with him, then come back six months later and it still would be the same. He would be walking around the stable area, bent almost in half over an aluminum crutch under his right arm. Arthritis has his back bowed and hardened so that he looks like a man carrying a beer keg on his back. He would keep looking up to see ahead of him and he would snap orders to stablehands taking care of the 45 valuable thoroughbreds under his command. Then in the afternoon he would sit at his favorite spot along the rail and watch his horses run and win or lose he would not get excited. He was in the big money; as big as there is in sports. It was a life he had earned by spending years scratching for meal money.

It was a good life for Mr. Fitz. Every day of it. And on June 21, 1951, it all started to fall apart. The day didn't seem to be a bad one. It was a soft spring morning at Aqueduct, the horses were on the track and Mr. Fitz was along the rail watching them. The phone rang in the cottage and a boy yelled out that it was for Mr. Fitz. He walked to the cottage, grumbling about being bothered when he was in the middle of his work. He picked up the phone.

"Yes," he said.

A man's voice on the other end said he was a policeman and that he had just been called in because of a death in the house and he wasn't sure of who was who in the family but he did know that Sunny Jim Fitzsimmons, the horse trainer—well, his wife had just died and he had been told to call somebody at the stable here and tell them.

It was as simple as that. When Mr. Fitz got home there was a police car and an ambulance in front of the house and inside there was a doctor who was saying, in the gentle tones they always use at such times, that it had been very quick; a heart attack; no pain; just one of those things that happens very quickly . . . at her age, you know. Jennie Fitzsimmons, Mr. Fitz's brick, was dead in her room upstairs. There was nothing to do but call the undertaker.

William Woodward, the New York banker whose horses Mr. Fitz had trained for over a quarter century, died during this period, too. Woodward had become a friend of Mr. Fitz's; the anything-goes kind of friend that you can only have after years of close association. Then George (Fish) Tappen, who had grown up with Mr. Fitz, died. Fish had been a part of Mr. Fitz's racing life for all but one or two years of his career. And the Bradys, who for twenty years kept house for Mr. Fitz, also died. Oh, maybe there was six months before Woodward went and another six months or so might have passed before Tappen and the Bradys went. But to Mr. Fitz it seemed like everything had turned into a dark blue suit and the smell of flowers they put around a casket, and the life he had worked for so hard was disappearing around him.

People who live to be very old always say it is the easiest thing in the world to let go when your friends are going. And

17

once you let go and lose interest in what is going on, it doesn't take long for the end to come.

This seemed to some to be what was happening with Mr. Fitz. Or maybe they just thought it was happening because they were looking for it. Anyhow, he seemed to be thinking more about the past than the present or future, and this wasn't like his usual self.

Then some claimed it started to show in the horses. They pointed to the winnings being off. But who could be sure of the reason? There are an awful lot of ifs and buts and maybes in this game.

One thing you can say for sure. Circumstances had changed, too. When William Woodward, Sr., died in 1952 his son Bill took over the stable. Through most of his life, the young Woodward had been around the horses only sparingly. Now he became interested in them and after spending a few days at the stable, then watching horses run in races, he was getting the feeling a man always gets when he is around good horses. Mr. Fitz thought he was a fine boy. But Mr. Fitz was seventy-seven and he had had twenty-seven years of working with a man he had come to think of as a friend and now he had to start all over again with somebody else. It was not easy.

Then something really did happen, and it made all the difference. On his last trip to Belair Stud with Woodward, Sr., Mr. Fitz had looked over the crop of weanlings, leggy little things with almost no bodies to them at all, and Woodward pointed to one of them and said that if everything went well this was a horse he wanted to send to the races in England.

"He is by Nasrullah out of Segula," Woodward said. "I like the breeding."

"He looks fine," Mr. Fitz said.

The next year Woodward was dead, his son was in charge and all of the racing was to be in America. One bright afternoon in the early fall, the young Woodward and Mr. Fitz were in a car which turned into the gravel driveway, bordered by fieldstone fence, of Belair Stud Farm. They were going to look at the yearlings which were about to be broken for racing and the weanlings which still had a year to go before this could be done.

At one enclosure, Woodward and Mr. Fitz got out and walked to the fence rail to look at a group of horses—mares, each with a weanling. When you are at a horse farm and you stand at a rail like this, you rap on the wood to make a noise and then one by one the mares and their yearlings lope toward you. If the weanling gets too close to these strangers at the fence, the mare sticks her head between the weanling and the fence and pushes her offspring away from the strangers he is too small to deal with. Now and then one of the weanlings will dart away from a mare, move as fast as he can in one jumble of long legs, then stop, flick the hind legs up in a little kick, wheel again, get the jumble of legs going, then dart back and put his head under the mare's stomach for a coffee break. You can watch them running around like this for hours.

If Sunny Jim needed a lift at this time in his life, it might well come from these fenced-in fields of soft dirt and deep grass with young horses running in them. Through all of his years, he had taken care of horses, good ones and bad ones, sound ones and ones with injuries nobody else wanted to bother with, and they had shaped his life. Maybe what he needed now, without even knowing it, was to have a big one going for him. The kind of horse that can put that little extra bit of excitement inside you. What was needed, simply was a horse that could make it a fair test between Sunny Jim Fitzsimmons and the calendar. The horse was in the next field.

He was a big, sturdy-legged, inquisitive yearling who came to the fence as Mr. Fitz and Woodward walked up, then wheeled and pounded back toward the center of the field, his feet sending clods of dirt into the air. He would not be two years old until the end of the year, but he had a chest on him and his legs looked like they could kick their way through a brick wall. You look at a horse such as this and it does something to you, even if you are not used to seeing horses. And

19

Mr. Fitz looked at him and asked Woodward which one was that colt out there.

"You saw him with my father," Woodward said. "He's by Nasrullah out of Segula. That's the one my father wanted to send to England."

"Oh, yes," Mr. Fitz said. "Good-lookin' kind of a colt. Good runnin' action. Look at that. Uses two leads at this stage. Big, too. Gonna be extra big. Oh, you can see he could be a real useful horse. Course you don't know what's inside him. Heart, lungs. You don't know that. But he looks real nice right now, don't he?"

"We have him nominated for everything," Woodward said.

"That's good. You never can tell."

Then they left and Mr. Fitz went back to New York to take care of his horses, but on the way back he was thinking a little bit about the horse. There was this one double-sized stall he had at Aqueduct. It used to be two stalls, but he had broken it into one for Johnstown. Remember that? Sure. Johnstown couldn't fit in an ordinary stall. Still got that extra big stall. Yes, it would be a good place to put this colt when he came to the track. He'd need it. You could see he was going to grow into a real big-sized horse. He had wide hips. Good, wide head, too. Plenty of spirit to him. Looked like he wanted to take your shoulder off. He walked with a little swagger, too. Didn't mope around, sloppy-like. Well, I've been wrong before lookin' at horses like this. So has everybody else. There's only one way to tell, though. Get him to racin' and see what happens. You won't know for a long time. This one seems to have something you could go to work on, though.

So he began to think ahead again, to the day when he would get this colt on the race track and see what could be done with him. This was 1953 and he was seventy-nine, but now he definitely had something to keep him going.

Woodward named the horse Nashua. You could stick your fist down the horse's throat, down to where the jaw comes out of the neck, and there would be plenty of room for it because this was a horse with a big windpipe and he could take in enough air to run for a month. He was sent out to a Westbury, Long Island, horse farm owned by John (Shipwreck) Kelly. Bill McCleary, one of Mr. Fitz's exercise boys, went out there to break the horse for racing. This was only the fall and it would be months before Nashua got to the races and the first year wouldn't be that important because a lot of times a horse doesn't come around until he is three years old. This is what makes being with horses beautiful. You are always waiting for something in the future and now, as Nashua learned how to get into a starting gate and how to run around turns, Mr. Fitz was waiting and looking ahead.

The stable shipped to Florida and in February, at Hialeah, he had Nashua on the track working. People saw the horse and they asked Mr. Fitz about him. The answer was what it should be.

"Like him?" Mr. Fitz said. "I don't know whether I like him or not. He's only a baby and we got a long way to go. He looks like he might be a good one, but how do I know? I can't tell if there's anything wrong with him. He can't tell me, either. He can't talk, you know. And I can't see inside him to find out what kind of a motor he's got. I hope he's good. But I don't know what he's going to be." He then kept on with an old-time Fitzsimmons monologue on horses and life and how little anybody knows about what's going to happen. After he was through, he gave a groom hell for throwing out too much straw while mucking out a stall and he was making demands on everybody else around him and that crutch was banging onto the ground hard when he walked. He was not interested in what happened yesterday.

Later in the year, in October, after Nashua had won several races and had lost a couple because he was green and ran that way, Mr. Fitz was standing in the infield at Belmont Park with his son John and grandson Jimmy and far up to the right Eddie Arcaro was sitting quietly on Nashua after they finished a warm-up and the horse was walking toward the start-

ing gate. The race was the Futurity. It was to be run on a strip
known as the Widener Chute. This was a running strip which
bisected the main track. The horses would come straight down
it to the finish line, with no turns. Because of the chute's angle
to the stands, it was nearly impossible for anybody in the
crowd to make out who was ahead in a race. Mr. Fitz had
always watched Futurities down the chute and it didn't bother
him. He knew what to look for.

When the race went off, he saw what he wanted. There
were good horses in this race . . . a horse called Summer Tan,
another called Royal Coinage, a good sprinter named King
Hairon, and he could be tough because the race was only for
six furlongs. They all came down fast. Mr. Fitz stood quietly,
with the crutch under his right arm. He watched the field as
it moved along. Halfway down the chute, somewhere around
the pole that said there were three furlongs left, Nashua let it
go. His stride became longer. His head stuck out. He was
working now. Running like a big one. The horses around
started to slip back. Then a little growl came from the bottom
of Mr. Fitz's throat. Then he growled again.

"Look at how he lowers his belly and goes to work," Mr.
Fitz said. There was a spark in his voice. The years had no
meaning to them now. This was Sunny Jim Fitzsimmons, age
anything, and he had a big horse.

Nashua slammed down the chute and won by a long neck.
Arcaro, a big grin on his face, brought the horse back to the
winner's circle. Woodward was there and so were the photographers and there were big trophies for everybody, and Arcaro
was saying that this big dude is a real runner.

Mr. Fitz was walking out of the infield. A brown-uniformed
Pinkerton swung open a part of the rail so he could walk
through and as Mr. Fitz came up the Pinkerton said, "Con-
gratulations, Mr. Fitz. Looks like a real good one, doesn't he?"

"Thank you. Oh, he looked all right today. But we got a
long way to go, you know. I want to get back to the barn and
see what he looks like right now."

Mr. Fitz walked through the gap onto the track and headed for the car in the parking lot so John could drive him back to the barn and he could have the groom walk Nashua around in front of him so he could look close and make sure the horse came out of it all right. Then he would sit down and watch them rub the sweat off the horse and cool him out with water and he'd have plenty of orders to give. No, he was certainly not going into the winner's circle. The barn was his winner's circle.

And as Mr. Fitz made his way across the track, Slim Sully leaned against the iron rail around the crowded winner's circle and looked at Nashua. Then Sully pointed over to Mr. Fitz and he smiled.

"Look at him," Sully was saying. "In what other business could an eighty-year-old man win something called the Futurity?"

Everybody used the line the next day in the papers. It was more than just a line. Mr. Fitz, they knew then, had a future going for him after that race and because of this, when you talk to a friend of Mr. Fitz's today about Nashua, the friend will smile a little and talk a lot about the horse and remember a lot of things about him. All of them will. Nobody ever will forget the part Nashua played in Mr. Fitz's life.

2. A Mistake . . . and a Big Day

With Nashua, Mr. Fitz, at eighty, started what amounted to another career. It was to lead to what is, as far as winning a horse race goes, the most important single victory of life. It came in 1955, when Nashua was a three-year-old. And it started with Mr. Fitz making a mistake.

Nashua had rolled up the field in important races in Florida early that year, winning the Flamingo at Hialeah and the Florida Derby at Gulfstream. In April, at Jamaica race track, he hooked up with Summer Tan in the Wood Memorial, run two weeks before the Derby. Nashua nearly filled hospitals that day. With Eddie Arcaro suspended for a riding infraction, Ted Atkinson was on Nashua. Atkinson was on a lot of horses and in a lot of tough races in his years. But the ride he had on Nashua in the Wood Memorial was something he can recall today, step for step. It made that kind of an impression on him. When he retired and wrote a book, Ted spent a whole chapter telling of the race.

Nashua started off by nearly throwing Atkinson while they were going to the gate. At the start he boiled out first, then sloughed off, and Summer Tan, with Eric Guerin up, took the lead. A good lead, too. He had a couple of lengths on Nashua. He wouldn't give it up, either. The rest of the horses in the race meant nothing as Nashua chased Summer Tan around the turn, all down the backstretch, around the turn again and into the stretch. With an eighth of a mile left, it was Summer Tan's race. With a sixteenth of a mile left, it was Summer Tan. Nashua started to pick it up a little, but it was too late. John Fitzsimmons was standing in the infield, behind the mutuel board, watching them come down. When they ran in front of the mutuel board and he couldn't see them any more, he put his head down. That's that, he said. There were only 70 yards left in the race when the horses went out of his view. There was no way for Summer Tan to lose. Even today, when you sit and watch a movie of the race, you would reach into your pocket and take out money and bet it that Nashua isn't going to catch Summer Tan when they are 70 yards from the wire.

But he caught him. With about seven whopping lunges, Nashua cut down the distance between Summer Tan and himself. Each one of them edged that nose closer to Summer Tan. Then with one swoosh, Nashua went under the wire a nose in front. In the stands, people dropped cigarettes. Eddie Arcaro, watching the race up on the roof, yelped.

"He win it, didn't he?" he shouted to people with him. "He win it, didn't he?"

It was the same in the jockeys' room. The little guys who ride horses and accept thrills as being commonplace were hopping around and shouting to one another. There had not been this kind of excitement over a horse race for fifteen years.

"He drew it kind of close, didn't he?" Mr. Fitz kidded people. Then he had John drive him home. It was a great win. Now he proceeded to make a mistake that he always talks about. He wants to make sure he punishes himself for it.

Mr. Fitz made arrangements for Nashua, the sure champion, to be shipped to Churchill Downs for the 1955 running of the Kentucky Derby with groom Al Robertson, exercise boy Bill McCleary, stable foreman Bart Sweeney, and John Fitzsimmons. Jockey Eddie Arcaro would be down the day before the Derby. Trainer James E. Fitzsimmons would stay at home and handle the whole thing over the telephone. The trip to Louisville didn't interest him at all. As he puts it, after all, what good can I do down there? The horse just needs a little breezing and then it's up to him and Arcaro. I can see the race on television better than I can at the track down there. It'll save me a long trip.

"I don't ship too good any more," he told everybody.

Mr. Fitz didn't know much about the other horses in the race, but he didn't see how that mattered. Summer Tan was the tough one. He had to be watched. There was this horse named Swaps from the coast, but fellows who were around horses told Mr. Fitz that Swaps was a good mile or a mile-and-an-eighth horse, not the kind of a horse who would be strong enough for the mile-and-a-quarter Derby. Distance, of course, was Nashua's game. He figured to be strongest of all at the end.

The night before the race, Mr. Fitz was on the phone with Arcaro. "Cater to Summer Tan," he said.

The next afternoon, in an office at Belmont Park, Mr. Fitz sat and watched the Kentucky Derby on television. Eddie Arcaro followed his orders perfectly. He stayed off the pace, which was set by Swaps, and kept looking for Summer Tan. He looked for Summer Tan on the backstretch. He looked for Summer Tan into the final turn. Willie Shoemaker, his rear end up in the air as he coasted along, had Swaps moving freely. He was saving plenty of the horse. At the top of the stretch, Arcaro looked for Summer Tan again. He still couldn't find him. So he started after Swaps. He got to Swaps all right. He lapped onto him at the eight pole. Shoemaker, with plenty of horse under him, now set Swaps down. The California horse had a big kick in him. He simply ran away to win by a length and a quarter.

Down in Louisville, Mr. Fitz's grandchildren, Kathleen and Jimmy, had tears in their eyes. But in Belmont Park, Mr. Fitz said simply, "I'm sorry for the horse that he lost. Don't be too hard on him. You know, I figure I chucked it for him."

Without making any long speeches he made sure everybody knew he had made a mistake. As bad as a man can make. Then he went home and watched television. But this was one lose, as they say, that he was not going to take easily.

After the race, Swaps was shipped back to California. Nashua went on to win the Preakness and the Belmont, but it didn't seem to matter. All you read about was Swaps. This was the California wonder horse. He was owned by Rex Ellsworth, a cow rancher, and trained by Mesach Tenney. Ellsworth and Tenney wore Levis, said horses were stupid animals and all this extra treatment people give race horses is a waste because they don't need it. This was completely opposite from anything Mr. Fitz ever had done. When Swaps came back from a workout, Tenney and Ellsworth were saying, they used a water hose on him, then let him dry in the sun and put him in the stall. Rubbing? That's for humans. This is a dumb animal. All horses are.

"He has his hay and grain and a good bed to sleep on," Tenney said. "The same as with humans, anything else you give him may be detrimental."

Mr. Fitz said nothing. Swaps was the wonder horse, he was being trained in a new modern way, and he had beaten Nashua. What could you say?

In July, Nashua was shipped to the Arlington Classic in Chicago, which he won. Swaps was scheduled to come to Washington Park on August 20 for the American Derby. Since both owners, Woodward and Ellsworth, were not against shipping to Chicago for normal races, it gave a couple of people ideas.

One was actor Don Ameche. He had been at race tracks betting horses through most of his adult life. He knew Ellsworth from the Coast. He also knew publicity-conscious Ben Lindheimer, owner of Chicago's Washington Park. It was a simple idea: put Swaps and Nashua in a match race. Lindheimer went for it. Ameche contacted Woodward and Ellsworth. Everybody agreed. The date was set for Wednesday,

August 31. It would be $100,000, winner take all, at a mile and a quarter.

They unloaded Nashua from a train at Saratoga on July 18, a Monday, and Mr. Fitz was there waiting for him. He now had a little over five weeks to get Nashua ready for the race of his life. He talked quietly and never made much of what was going on.

Nashua was muscled up, as Mr. Fitz says, when he started working for the match race. So he simply had the horse lumbering along on the deep training track, called the Oklahoma at Saratoga, putting in a two-mile gallop, then another, then a mile gallop, with no particular time called for. Then in August he sent Nashua three-quarters of a mile in 1:17 2/5 and then another three-quarters in 1:15. These are racing times and most people don't know what they mean, but as Mr. Fitz sat in his stable office and looked at the typewritten workbook for Nashua and checked the times each day and then planned for the next, the figures were his life. They meant everything to him. He was pointing the horse for one thing: he wanted Nashua to be screw-tight on August 31 and he wanted to have the horse throw the fastest first three-quarters of a mile possible. It was a match race at a mile and a quarter, but every match race he had ever seen in all his years on the race track was strictly a test of speed from the start. "Make the other horse crack," he kept saying.

Arcaro agreed, even to the extent that his fellow jockey, Con McCreery, voiced wonder at the fact that Eddie was practicing starts as a green kid would in the week before the match race.

The arrangements called for Nashua to be shipped to Washington Park on Friday, August 26. On the Saturday before that, August 19, Mr. Fitz was sitting in a folding chair under a big tree in the paddock at Saratoga and only a couple of people were around him. The crowd walking around the tree-shaded paddock was clustered about the horses who were being saddled for the next race, looking for betting informa-

29

tion. When the horses went out for the race, the fourth of the afternoon, everybody followed them and the place was empty except for Mr. Fitz and a couple of sports writers who were talking to him. This was good, because then you could see, with no crowding, something you would remember all your life.

From the stable area, coming in the same way they bring a heavyweight champion into the ring, four grooms walked Nashua toward Mr. Fitz. Al Robertson led him. Then there was a groom named Chico and another one named Andy and exercise boy Bill McCleary. They all had towels and were waving them around Nashua to keep the flies away.

"The last time I saw anybody come in like this it was Dempsey getting into the ring at Chicago," somebody said to Mr. Fitz.

"Well, he's a nice horse and there's a lot of flies around here and I kind of like to treat a horse right," Mr. Fitz said. But he had a little smile. This is the big leagues, son, the smile said.

Eddie Arcaro, in a white T-shirt and riding pants, walked up to Mr. Fitz, leaned over and talked to the old man. Then he threw his cigarette away, put the toe of his boot into Robertson's cupped hand and hopped up onto Nashua's back with that little feather motion jockeys have.

Arcaro started walking Nashua toward the track. When the fourth race was over, Eddie and Nashua came on and Freddy Capposella, the public address announcer, said that Nashua was now on the track for his last public workout before going to Chicago to face Swaps in the match race of the century. Arcaro and Nashua lumbered along in front of the stands, moved around the turn, and on the backstretch Eddie's rear end came down and his arms started to pump and Nashua took off. There is a teletimer on the mutuel board which gives the time for the race as it progresses and it started to click off as Nashua moved. Clockers were catching it, too. Only they were breaking it down into fractions for each eighth of a

30

mile, and as Nashua moved, they caught him and after a couple of furlongs they started talking.

"Eleven and a fifth," Frenchy Schwartz said. "Eleven and three fifths. Eleven and four fifths. Oh, what is he doing with this horse? This is time for a sprint champ. He's supposed to be getting ready for a mile and a quarter. There you go again. Twelve and two . . . Thirteen . . . Twelve and four. This is crazy."

Out on the track, Arcaro was a white piece of Nashua's motion and as they moved the big crowd began to start a loud *Oooooh!* Then it became louder and now it was a roar as Nashua busted down the backstretch and into the turn. Arcaro kept him going and the people kept yelling until Arcaro eased up and Nashua slowed down for the rest of the work. You didn't have to know a thing about racing. It could have been your first time at the races. It didn't matter. You knew this horse was running like hell.

After the workout, Arcaro brought Nashua back to Mr. Fitz and he was not just a guy coming from a workout.

"How'd it go, Eddie?" Mr. Fitz called up to him.

Arcaro jumped down and almost shouted. "Wonderful," he said. "Just wonderful, Mr. Fitz."

He was a little excited now and he turned to the other people and said, "Maybe that other horse is a super horse, like they say. If he is, then forget it. But if he's just another real good race horse, then he's going to have some time with this dude."

The grooms had a white blanket over Nashua and one of them was giving him some water to drink and the others kept shooing away flies. At the stable they would rub him down with liniment, cool him out, and treat him as if he were royalty. That was Mr. Fitz's way to train a race horse.

Clockers and racing writers didn't know about that. They thought Mr. Fitz had lost the touch.

"I don't know what it is," Bill Corum wrote, "but he is ruining this horse's chance. He is training him for a six-furlong sprint and out in Chicago that machine from the Golden Slopes of the West is oiled up for the same mile and a quarter distance that found Nashua wanting in the Kentucky Derby."

Mr. Fitz shrugged. On August 24, Nashua was put into a private car attached to the New York Central's *Pacemaker*, with Mr. Fitz following a couple of days later.

There had not been a horse race in years to produce such interest. The track was filled with television people and newspapermen from all over the country in the days before the race. They talked about what the horses ate, what their habits were, what they did each day. But mostly they wrote about the new and the old of racing—the Ellsworth-Tenney way to take care of a horse and get him ready, and the old way of Mr. Fitz. They made a lot out of it and nearly everybody was picking Swaps to run off and hide. That was all right with Mr. Fitz. Two days before the race, when he looked at Nashua, he didn't think there was anything alive which could beat him.

Al Robertson walked Nashua around the infield turf course and in front of the crowded stands that day for a rehearsal of their saddling procedure. The horses were to be saddled in the infield, in front of the stands, and Mr. Fitz wanted the horse to get used to the new surroundings. In the middle of the walk, Nashua stopped. He looked around. Then he went right up into the air on his hind legs, his mane tossing, his head high, tugging at Robertson's grip on the reins. Robertson held him tight, then got him to come down. A few yards later, Nashua did it again. He came down, walked a while, then went up again. He did this four times and he had the groom scared stiff.

"If he does it again, he'll go right over backwards," Robertson said.

"That's his idea of playin'," Mr. Fitz said. "He rares up when he wants to play. I don't like that. He could get hurt. Keep a good holt on him."

When they got Nashua back to the barn safely, both Robertson and Mr. Fitz could relax. And smile a little. They knew what the rearing up meant. This was a horse who was so fit he was bursting with energy he had to get rid of.

The race was for Wednesday afternoon. It rained on Monday night and kept right on raining through Tuesday. On Wednesday, papers all over the country had stories about the race and it was all you heard of around Chicago. The tension was all over the track as the match race of the century was about to be held on a muddy track that was drying in spots.

At noontime, Frank Graham said to Red Smith, a columnist friend of his, "Let's walk over and wish Mr. Fitz luck."

"Oh, no," Smith said. "Don't go near him now. We better leave him alone. The last thing they'll want around is people."

"Just for a minute," Graham said.

He and Smith walked quietly and solemnly to Barn A, went down the shedrow and stepped into the tack room at the end of the barn to see Mr. Fitz. They went as solemnly as if they were in a church. And Mr. Fitz, the nervous man who needed quiet, was sitting with John and they both were eating sandwiches and having a glass of milk. Mr. Fitz looked up at the visitors and said, "Why didn't you tell us you were coming around? We'd of gotten a sandwich for you. Well, it's too late for you now. I'm going to eat this and then I'm going to roll right over on that cot and take a nap for myself and you can take this damn match race of yours and do anything you want with it. I'm going to take a nap."

Then he joked with Graham and Smith and they left. They thought it was hard to believe. And Mr. Fitz took his nap. Later, at 5 P.M., he was in the infield, Nashua alongside him. Eddie Arcaro came out and the two of them walked off by themselves a little and Eddie, his arms folded, listened to Mr. Fitz. They both talked about what to do.

"Just keep Swaps busy," Mr. Fitz said. "If Swaps gets off first, you go right after him. Don't let him take it easy at all. Run from the jump. You should be all right."

Arcaro nodded. Then he unfolded his arms and went over and got on Nashua and Mr. Fitz tugged at his bowtie and started walking across the track to a box seat they had set up for him.

A little earlier, in the red brick convent of St. Benedict Joseph Labre Church on 118th Street in Richmond Hill, Long Island, the sister superior had mentioned to one of her nuns that Mrs. Dolan, who lived over on 114th Street, was sick and should be visited. The sister superior was a great believer in the corporal works of mercy. And while you're going, the sister superior said, you might bring Sister Anella with you. She almost said, bring Sister Nashua with you, which is what everybody else in the convent was calling Mr. Fitz's granddaughter.

Mrs. Dolan, on 114th Street, was most assuredly not well, but by the same token she also was not at death's door. So she thought a little television might be nice while the two sisters from St. Benedict's visited her. The best program being televised at this hour happened to be the Swaps-Nashua race from Chicago. So as Eddie Arcaro took his big guy to the post at Washington Park, Sister Anella sat on the floor in front of Mrs. Dolan's TV set in the living room in Richmond Hill and held out her fingers so she could start snapping them the minute the race began.

On the parade to the post, Arcaro kept tugging at the reins, getting a feel of Nashua and then looking down at the track. There were paths in it. These are patches of solid footing you can find in a race track here and there among the rows of mud when a track is drying a little. He kept looking at the paths and thinking about them. Before this race, to most people, Arcaro had been taking a back seat to Willie Shoemaker, and if there is one thing that makes Eddie Arcaro go, it is pride. No man is going to take the play away from Arcaro if it involves riding race horses. He kept looking at those paths.

The starting gate was out on the track now and, as an assistant starter took hold of Nashua and led him into stall No. 2, Eddie looked at the ground. Stall No. 3 was empty. There was a path running straight out from No. 3. Swaps was in No. 4. Get out there first and grab that path, Arcaro said to himself.

34

Both horses got into the gate. The assistant starter crouched on the gate alongside Arcaro, then got out of the way. Nashua was fine. Arcaro hunched forward. He held his whip up in his right hand. The minute the gate opened he was going to bang Nashua and get him running from the jump. There wasn't a sound in the stands as they waited for the gates to open.

Then the bell rang and the gates were open and before the crowd could make noise you could hear Arcaro scream. He was shrieking at Nashua as the gate opened and he brought the whip down in a crack. Nashua banged out onto the track and Arcaro seesawed the reins and dropped Nashua's head right over the good running path in front of stall No. 3. Shoemaker came out on Swaps and was amazed to see Nashua had broken first. He thought Nashua's run would be strictly from behind and later in the race. Willie headed Swaps for the path, but Nashua was already there, so Willie had to swing his horse to the right a little. Then he had to go about the business of trying to keep up with Nashua. That was the hardest of all. For this was a horse as fit as human hands could make him and Nashua simply burned down the stretch the first time and Arcaro kept forcing Shoemaker to go wide. As they went into the backstretch Swaps came to Nashua. No good. Nashua pulled away. Farther down he came up again and they were even for a few strides but Nashua lowered his belly and drew out by three parts of a length. The pace was killing. They went five eighths of a mile in 58 seconds. They did three quarters of a mile in 1:10 2/5. This was the kind of time Nashua had been trained for and he was taking it all out of Swaps. At the head of the stretch Swaps came on again, but Mr. Fitz was watching the shadows of the horses as they fell on the infield.

"He ain't closin' much," he said. "Them shadows ain't together."

Swaps did not close. Swaps was through at the head of the stretch and Nashua began to open it up. A length and a half. Then two. Then three, four, and now Arcaro had lost his head.

35

He was switching the whip from one hand to the other and slamming it into Nashua and kicking and riding as if this were a head-and-head duel. He was six lengths ahead and still whipping as he went under the wire.

"Excited," Mr. Fitz said. "I did the same thing myself when I won my first race."

Back in Richmond Hill, Long Island, everybody on 114th Street could hear a loud shriek which came from Mrs. Dolan's house, where the two Sisters of St. Joseph were visiting.

"He *won* it!"

After the ceremonies in the winner's circle, which, for once, Mr. Fitz had to be in on, he headed back for the barn and looked closely. Nashua was being walked in a circle inside a paddock and a boy was walking Swaps behind him.

"How's your horse?" Robertson asked the boy with Swaps.

"Fine. Just got beat," the boy said.

Mr. Fitz grunted. Later, when the story came out in the papers that Swaps had suffered a foot injury somewhere during the race, Mr. Fitz snorted. Anybody who asked him about it received a gentle play-by-play of how Swaps was well enough during the race to run 1:10 and 2/5 for the first three-quarters and he wasn't getting ahead of Nashua. You don't do that with a bad foot, he pointed out.

This race was in 1955. Since then both Nashua and Swaps have retired to stud and so has Mr. Fitz's next big horse, Bold Ruler, and there have been more races and more horses since then. You thought about that last summer when Mr. Fitz was showing somebody the horses along the shedrow at Belmont Park. Mr. Fitz pointed to one and said, "This one's named Tit for Tat. Colt by Swaps. Wish he were by Nashua."

"Oh, yes," the man said. "That was the big match race, wasn't it? When was that now?"

"Back in '55," Mr. Fitz said.

Then Mr. Fitz took the man to another stall and showed him a filly named Auction Block.

"Always something the matter with her," Mr. Fitz was saying. "We got her vaccinated to be a real good runner but so far it ain't took. Keeps hurtin' her back or one of her legs. But she'll be all right. Only a little two-year-old, you know. She got time. Plenty of time. Later on this year. Should be fine for next year, too."

Then Mr. Fitz walked away and he was thinking about next year. I don't know whether there is going to be a next year and neither does he nor anybody else, but that's all Mr. Fitz thinks about now and as long as he is like this you always have a good feeling when you are around him because you know he is everything that he always has been and that makes him one extra special human being.

3. The Man

You are never supposed to find anyone who is famous living around the corner from a place like Harry's, for Harry's is a bar and grill on Cross Bay Boulevard in the Ozone Park section of New York City. Ozone Park is a place where working people live and Harry's is a bar with twelve stools, a TV, and a picture window which looks out onto a bus stop. It does not seem to be anything special at all, but it is important because it is the place where you stop in and get cigarettes and a couple of drinks before going around to 91-41 Chicot Court, which is where you can find Mr. Fitz whenever he isn't working at the track. Mr. Fitz has never really figured out what to do with success; he's still working on the subject of what success actually means and when he has that straightened out he'll take up the matter of how to live with it. So he sits to one side, around the corner from Harry's, and when you get to know him, as we are going to try to do here, you will see that he is a beautiful person.

His house on Chicot Court is a small, six-room place that is the same as every other house on the block except for the color of its shingles, red. It has a cement back yard hardly large enough to accommodate a dice game. The narrow driveway defies you to bring a car in without scraping the house next door. Two tiny plots of grass border the brick stoop in front. The first time we ever saw him, we had been sent out to interview him for a newspaper story. He is one of the most written-about people in sports and it came as a shock to find the famous subject sitting in shorts in a smallish living room that was furnished no better and no worse than that of a cop working out of the nearby 105th Precinct. A Pontiac, four or five years old at the time, was in front of the house. His simple style of living was brought up during the interview; for the first few moments we had the crazy idea that we were talking to the wrong guy, that this was a retired city worker. Mr. Fitz gave a little snort when his circumstances were brought up.

"Let me tell you something, son," he said. "Them fellas that flash things around don't get anything out of it except a lot of bills. Doesn't mean a thing. Doesn't make you any better than the next guy, but it might go to your head and make you worse. Besides, what more does a man need than something to eat, a roof over his head, a family that loves him and a clean set of underwear every day?"

With Sunny Jim Fitzsimmons, it is always like this. He has a way of reducing anything down to a simple little bit of living. The bigger the thing, the smaller Mr. Fitz makes it. A cold, damp afternoon in Louisville, Kentucky, is as good a place as any to start showing you this.

It was the first Saturday in May of 1957 and by 4:30 in the afternoon, which was when Tom Young walked out in front of the stands at Churchill Downs race track, the sky had no color except flat gray. Young walked to the middle of the track, then stopped and looked at his wristwatch. When it was 4:37, he took the gray hat from his head, waved it, then brought it down and held it over his heart. A uniformed bandmaster, who was standing in the track's infield, saw the signal. He held up his baton, gave the downbeat and the band started to play "My Old Kentucky Home." As the music made its first sounds into the cold air, a red-coated outrider came out of the tunnel from under the stands aboard a chestnut pony and after him came the fifteen horses who were going to run in the Kentucky Derby. The music was loud now and you could hear people in the wooden stands singing. The horses had sleek coats and as they came out they would scuff the neatly raked dirt, then dance a little on their thin legs. The jockeys would sway with the motion and now it wasn't a bad day at all because when the field for the Kentucky Derby comes on the track it is a thing that you never really can forget.

As this was going on, Mr. Fitz was walking from the paddock to the track. He was two months shy of being eighty-three on this day and bent with arthritis. Each year, the arthritis brings his head down a little more.

He was dressed in his best Kentucky Derby splendor: an old gray hat; a covert topcoat decorated with a little fraying around the pockets; slightly baggy pants; and high-top black shoes. He was a little out of the ordinary in the paddock, where mink, expensive tweeds and large diamonds were the order. But everybody made a point of saying hello to him and touching his hand as he moved along and when they would say, "How you, MistFitz?" he would smile, "Oh, I'm fine. I hope the horse's fit as I am."

The horse was Bold Ruler, a beautifully put together dark brown colt who was out on the track now with Eddie Arcaro, the jockey, sitting on his back. Arcaro's legs were drawn back, his shoulders were slumped and his hands were manipulating the reins while he studied Bold Ruler's reactions on the way to the starting gate. The odds board in the center of the infield showed Bold Ruler was the 8–5 favorite in this biggest of all races. Mr. Fitz remembered his mistake with Swaps two years earlier and was on hand for this one.

For Mr. Fitz, this was one of the most important days of his life. He was at an age where people are not supposed to be useful, but he was getting another chance at winning a Kentucky Derby. So he picked, as usual, a totally impossible place from which to watch the race. He came on the track and sat down on a small green folding chair which was set against a wire fence at the edge of the track. While everybody else important in this Derby was sitting upstairs, in a box seat where you could see and with people who had names you know, Mr. Fitz sat and listened to Dogwagon, who is an exercise boy for Calumet Farm.

Calumet had a horse named Iron Liege entered in the race and Dogwagon, whose life is mainly one of financial calamities, was worried because he had gone overboard betting on Iron Liege.

"You goin' take the bread out of Dogwagon's mouth today, MistFitz?" he said.

"You shouldn't bet, son," Mr. Fitz said. He waved his hand at some others who were around him. "Nobody should bet. Lose your money that way."

"Mah bill collectors know all about that," Dogwagon said.

"Are you a little nervous?" another who was standing alongside Mr. Fitz asked.

"Yes, I'm worried about how much drinkin' you been doing down here all week. I'm afraid that wife of yours is going to throw you out of the house."

Far up the track, to the left, flashes of color started to appear in the starting gate. They were the bright silks of the jockeys who were already in the gate with their horses. Khaki-wearing assistant starters were hustling around, leading the horses into the gate, then hopping up onto it to help the riders keep their horses still so they would be standing straight when the gate opened and the race went off. The track announcer's voice on the loudspeaker said, "It is now post time," and the big crowd was quiet because the horses would be coming out on any breath now. Then the gates opened and the horses flashed onto the track and the crowd put a blanket of noise over the place.

From where Mr. Fitz sat it was impossible to tell who was in front until the pack came almost up to him. When they did, Bold Ruler was on the lead, with a horse named Federal Hill a head behind and on the outside Bill Hartack, the jockey, was pushing Iron Liege into close quarters with the other two. Then the horses were gone and far down at the end of the straightway they went around the first turn and there was no way to see after that. The crowd of ten thousand in the infield blocked all view of anything that was happening on the other side of the track.

Mr. Fitz turned and watched the pari-mutuel board and tried to listen to the race track announcer's call. But when the lights started to blink and showed that first Federal Hill and then Iron Liege took the lead the crowd made so much noise you couldn't hear the announcer. Then Mr. Fitz turned and strained his neck to look up the track again where the horses would be coming into view again as they entered the stretch.

You could make out Arcaro's purple and yellow silks right away when the field came off the turn. Arcaro's right arm rose and fell in a steady motion as he hit Bold Ruler with the whip, but it was no good. Bold Ruler's legs were moving as if he were on an escalator.

It is as bad a moment as you can ever have in sports. When a horse comes around the turn in the Kentucky Derby like this you can forget all the hard work and hope and money because the horse is going to do nothing but make your stomach empty. But Mr. Fitz just looked at the horse for a moment, then his blue eyes had the light of a smile in them and he turned to Captain Edward Byrne, who had come down from New York with him and now was standing next to him.

Cap's mouth had sagged open and his right hand was sticking into a pants pocket that was filled with pari-mutuel betting tickets on Bold Ruler.

"Got your carfare home, son?" Mr. Fitz said.

The two horses who were leading went by in a gunshot of noise and motion. This was Gallant Man and Iron Liege hooking up for one of the most famous Derby finishes of all. But down on the track they went by so quickly you couldn't tell who they were. The dirt flew in big pieces as their hoofs pounded the track and there was tremendous noise from the stands, but you still could hear the *whack-whack-whack* as the jockeys slammed away with the whips. A full sixteenth of a mile down the track they passed under the finish line and there was no way to tell who had won.

But Mr. Fitz said quietly, "See that? Gallant Man's jockey lost the race, right here in front of us. He took this pole here, the sixteenth pole, for the finish line. Stood up in the saddle and he loses it." The jockey was Willie Shoemaker. Iron Liege won the race and Dogwagon was screaming.

Bold Ruler had finished fourth and Arcaro stopped the horse in front of Mr. Fitz, flipped his baton to a valet, jumped down and didn't look one way or the other as he walked off to the jockeys' room.

Snag, who is a groom, was holding Bold Ruler and Bart Sweeney, the stable foreman, was putting a blanket over the horse's back when Mr. Fitz got up and walked in front of the horse and looked at him closely. Bold Ruler was breathing heavily, but evenly.

"Nothing the matter with him," Mr. Fitz said. "Just got beat, that's all." Then he smiled. "Well, let's get out of here. We got no time for foolin' around. We been down here havin' a vacation with one horse. I've got twenty-nine of them back in New York and I have to be up a little after five o'clock Monday morning to work 'em."

Then he walked off surprisingly fast for one in his condition. It was the craziest way to lose you ever saw. On this dark afternoon he had reduced the big, storied Kentucky Derby to a simple matter of sitting on a chair and watching a horse lose.

That night, New York's Idlewild Airport was a tangle of purple and red lights and the plane circled over it, then began to come at the blackness between two rows of the purple. The plane hit the runway with a bounce, the engine exhaust flaring orange, then purple, and then it taxied up to a terminal gate that was, mercifully for the Derby passengers debarking, only a few steps away from one of the airport bars.

The bartender had the early editions of the Sunday tabloids

44

in front of him and as he tumbled Scotch into glasses he talked about the race.

"That Shoemaker," he was saying. "He done something, didn't he? Imagine a top boy like that forgettin' himself. That was something."

"Shoemaker?" we said to him. "What did he have to do with it?"

"What did he do?" the bartender said. "Well, if you was in Louisville today and you don't know what Shoemaker done, then you must of been down there to visit relatives because everybody around here even knows what he done."

"No, I saw the race," we said to him. "It's just I was so busy watching Fitzsimmons I'm still thinking about him now. Tell you the truth, I forgot all about Shoemaker."

Mr. Fitz does that with all the other things that you usually think of as being important in life. The matter of being old, for example. With him it comes down to nothing more than a numbers game. His birthday, celebrated at two or three convenient times during the summer, comes in July. At eighty-seven, he feels he could be twenty years younger or older and it wouldn't make any difference. He is a man who learned to read and write and sharpen his mind by himself over the years and he has refused to let time do anything to change this. They make a big business of old age in this nation, but Mr. Fitz makes a shambles of the subject by working six days a week, fifty-two weeks of the year and snorting if you mention a vacation or rest.

One morning in 1960, at about the time of his eighty-sixth birthday, Mr. Fitz was around his horses at Belmont Park and a visitor was busy reading one of those "Golden Years" columns of advice to the aged which was in one of the papers.

"Did you read this?" he asked Mr. Fitz. "It's filled with advice for people who get old."

"Does it say in there that they should get off their fannies and go do a day's work?" Mr. Fitz said. "If it don't, it's wrong."

45

He has a bad physical affliction which has deformed his once stick-straight body and while most human beings react badly when something like this happens to them, Mr. Fitz has always considered it to be meaningless. Little by little, over the years, the arthritis has caused his stoop to be more pronounced, but it has never kept him from a day's work and, as he keeps saying, "I'm kind of lucky on it. I hear that some fellas that get it have a lot of pain and I don't know as I'd like that too much. I don't have any pain from it at all and it don't keep me from workin'. So there's no sense worryin' about it."

In his years he has seen about everything, and in his business, he has been with names which have become legends in financial and sports history, and he has been around some of them, such as Frank James of the James boys, who do not stand so well. But with an approach to life that you seldom find nowadays, Mr. Fitz doesn't think much of this at all. There are things that never show in the newspapers that he thinks of as far more urgent.

These problems keep him well occupied and thus unable to regard himself as famous. There is the matter of his family, for example. Mr. Fitz has two brothers, a sister, five children, seventeen grandchildren, and approximately thirty great-grand-children. This number cannot really be kept accurate because as the founder explains, "Somebody's always foalin'." Now this Irish-American answer to the Ming dynasty has a way of staying together which makes even a casual family gathering look like a protest meeting. Once, for a television program called "Person to Person" which was coming from Mr. Fitz's Sheepshead Bay house, the entire Fitzsimmons clan was gathered, but between the cameras, cables, technicians, and family there was no way to fit everybody in at the same time. So the family was outside, bread-line style, and whenever a camera moved out of the way a few more were dispatched inside to put their best scrubbed faces forward into living rooms around the country.

The family also has a way of enveloping outsiders which at times makes it difficult to determine anybody's status. When one person meets a Fitzsimmons he almost immediately meets all Fitzsimmonses and it is not long before he is being taken for some part of the family. There was one gloomy morning a few years ago at New York's Aqueduct race track when Cap Byrne was found outside the Fitzsimmons barn talking about this. The Cap, a retired New York City police captain, died in 1958. On this day he was, as usual, out at the track to be with his old friend Mr. Fitz for the workouts. But Mr. Fitz at 6:30 or so in the morning is much more like an old foreman than an old friend, and on this day he had given the stable crew, including sons John, sixty-five, and Jim, sixty-three, a general bawling out. The Cap was generously included.

"I finally had to tell him," Byrne muttered. "I had to tell him, 'Listen, I'm not a Fitzsimmons. Yell at them, not at me.'"

Mr. Fitz, since getting his first job on a race track seventy-six years ago, has done nothing else for a living. And during this time he has gotten the idea that there is little difference between horses and people, except that people talk, which many times would seem to give quite an edge to horses. Since the string of horses he trains, numbering anywhere from twenty-nine to forty-two, are considered by him to be the same as his family, he does not know their names. But, as he insists, he knows the breeding. So horses usually are called by their sire's name, such as the "Nasrullah colt."

He proved this one summer afternoon at Belmont Park when a groom came by, leading a horse from the tree-lined stable area out to the paddock to be saddled for the next race.

"Let me get a look at her, will you, son?" he asked.

"Sure thing, boss," the groom said. He stopped and tugged at the horse to keep its head up.

The old man was off to one side and his face crinkled into a little smile.

"Oh, I know this one all right," he said. "She's an Apache mare. I had her father. Ran him in the Kentucky Derby one year . . . 1940, I think it was. Well, I hope she does all right, son. I like to see horses do good and she's from a nice colt."

"How'd you do with 'Pache, MistFitz?" the groom asked.

"Oh, no good. Didn't get much of anything. Finished way up the track in the Derby."

"Then you worryin' 'bout this one? Ah'd be cussin' her and her father."

"Oh, I just like to see people I know do good. Well, good luck, son. Hope she wins the race."

"You want to know her name?"

"Oh, I'd only forget that. But don't worry, I know who she is."

Because of Mr. Fitz's outlook, it also is impossible for him to become excited when he wins a big race. In February 1955, for example, he sent Nashua out to run in the $100,000 Widener Handicap at Florida's Hialeah Park and it turned into a tremendous race.

Nashua, the big, strapping chunk of power had been purchased the year before by a syndicate headed by Leslie Combs II for a record price of $1,251,200. The Widener was Nashua's first start since the sale and the job of caring for over a million dollars' worth of horse, and trying to win some of the money back for his owners, should have been nerve-testing at best. Then there was the problem of bringing Nashua along without the benefit of a race and sending him into the tough Widener in the kind of condition that wins six-figure race purses. It looked like a tough order. Which it was. Nashua had to come on and win the way only the big ones do. In the last strides of a head-nodding, four-horse finish he got his nose in front and kept it there at the wire and knocked everybody dead with the kind of finish you don't forget.

1 Mr. Fitz as a jockey

2 Mr. Fitz riding in the
Oldtimers' Race at
Pimlico in the 1920s

3 Mr. Fitz, Rox Angarola and, center, Walter Miller, leading rider at the time, which was around 1914

4 Mr. Fitz and James Fitzsimmons, Jr., in the 1920s

5 Max Hirsch and Mr. Fitz (1959)

(The New York Times)

6 Gallant Fox winning
the Preakness in 1930
(Wide World Photos)

7 Omaha—"Smokey" Saunders up—
winner of 1935 Kentucky Derby
(International News Photo, Inc.)

8 Mr. Fitz, William Woodward, Sr., and
William Woodward, Jr. *(Turf Pix)*

9 Nashua and Swaps—right after the start of the match
race at Chicago, August 1955

10 Mr. Fitz and Nashua (1956)

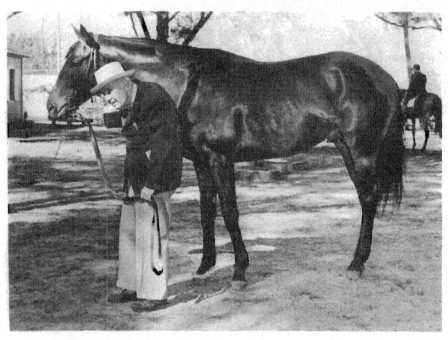

The late John McNulty, one of the finest of writers, watched this race over television at his New York apartment and Nashua's finish murdered him. There is always a tingle of excitement to the finish of a good race. But McNulty, at the time, was writing an article on Mr. Fitz for *Collier's* magazine and his particular interest in the race caused Nashua's finish to hit him like a thrown brick. Several cans of beer did nothing to quiet McNulty's nerves and that night he put in a long-distance call to Mr. Fitz, who was in his cottage near Hialeah.

"How are you, Mr. Fitz?" McNulty asked.

"Oh, I'm fine, son. How are you?" Mr. Fitz said.

"That was a wonderful race. What are you doing now?" McNulty asked.

"Oh, I'm mixing the breakfast batter right now," Mr. Fitz said. "I mix it half buckwheat and half pancake and then let it stand that way in the refrigerator overnight. The kids like it that way when I cook breakfast for 'em in the morning."

The kids were sons John and Jim, both of course, in their sixties. The proper pancake batter for them was quite important. McNulty went heavy on the beer that night trying to put the whole thing together.

For Mr. Fitz, everything starts at 6:15 each morning, whether in Florida or New York. Having made breakfast just for himself when he's home, Mr. Fitz starts down the walk at Chicot Court as his son Jim pulls to the curb in a car. At this hour, Mr. Fitz is dressed in two thick gray vests which, because of his stoop, hang down to his knees. A green nylon rain jacket is over them. His magnificent gray hat, the brim turned up now, covers his bald head. He always gets down the stoop, then turns around and fumbles with the mailbox. Finding it empty he turns and starts to the car—a little grumpily, because he feels people have become so lazy these days they don't even deliver the mail until half the morning is gone. Then he slips into the front seat of his son's 1956 Pontiac. Mr. Fitz, since his wife's death, lives during the week with a housekeeper in the Chicot Court house because it is only a couple of blocks away from Aqueduct and a twenty-minute drive to Belmont Park. His son John lives in the family homestead in Sheepshead Bay, Mr. Fitz's birthplace. His sons John and Jim take turns picking him up in the morning and the routine always is the same. The old man gets into the front seat, picks up the racing paper, *The Morning Telegraph,* and reads it during the short drive to Belmont Park.

It was this way one morning last fall. As the car swung into the stable entrance at Belmont Park, the Pinkerton guard on duty waved and walked over to the car to say hello. At the end of the short, tree-shaded street, Jim slowed the car and started to pull it into a parking space alongside a small wooden cottage which serves as the Fitzsimmons stable headquarters. The car was still moving but Mr. Fitz was fumbling with the door handle and Jim had to stop the car abruptly because Mr. Fitz was getting out whether the car had stopped or not.

"He never waits until I stop the thing," Jim said.

"I got to go to work," Mr. Fitz said. Then he was moving across the blacktop road to a long, green-painted Barn No. 17, which was alive with horses and men about to start a day of training for races.

Mr. Fitz has been getting up like this all his life. In his years he has come to handle some of the great race horses. In 1930 there was Gallant Fox, a horse which would run over anything in its way and won everything. He is still Mr. Fitz's favorite. Or, later in the '30s, there was Johnstown and Omaha. Then in recent times there was Nashua, who became such a favorite with the public that they wrote fan letters to him. And after Nashua was Bold Ruler, who didn't lose much else after that Kentucky Derby. In his time, Mr. Fitz has won three of those Derbys, along with some 225 winners of 95 other important stakes races. The total winnings come to something like $6,500,000 from those special stakes races alone. His numbers of winners in ordinary races is staggering. His record puts him one–two or thereabouts as the most successful trainer of horses in racing history.

Mr. Fitz today trains horses for four people, all of whom, or their families, have employed him for well over thirty years. The largest string of horses under his care is owned by Mrs. Henry Carnegie Phipps, a gentle, gray-haired lady in her seventies. Her son, Ogden Phipps, has a string of horses under Mr. Fitz's direction as do Whitney Stone and Mrs. Thomas Bancroft, a daughter of the late William Woodward, Sr., whose Belair Stud Farm was Mr. Fitz's biggest responsibility for twenty-nine years.

These people have money, which, if you want to own race horses, is as urgent as gin in the summer. The bills for horses in training under James E. Fitzsimmons come to about $400,000 a year. And the cost of breeding and raising these thoroughbreds on sprawling Kentucky and Virginia horse farms can be frightening. Mr. Fitz charges $14 a day for each horse he trains. Out of this he pays feed bills, stable salaries and the like. His personal income from this is negligible. Mr. Fitz's money comes from a 10 per cent cut of all money his horses earn. This arrangement can result in a warming bank balance when you handle the kind of horses Mr. Fitz has had. In three years of racing, for example, Nashua earned $1,288,565 and his trainer's cut was what many would consider a living.

There was for example the bright afternoon of October 30, 1956, when it seemed Mr. Fitz had come up with a way to solve recessions.

At a little after 3:30 that afternoon, Mr. Fitz leaned against the front of a car parked on the grass along the first turn at Belmont as Eddie Arcaro broke Nashua out of the gate in the two-mile Jockey Club Gold Cup. First money in the race was $87,500 and Nashua's brutal strength wore out everything trying to run with him and he set a new world record for the distance. As they led Nashua off the track, Mr. Fitz made his way back to the paddock where he watched closely as they put a saddle on Bold Ruler, who was to run in the next race, the historic and always rich Futurity. Mr. Fitz again

stationed himself against the automobile and watched as Bold
Ruler came out of the gate with a rush. There seemed to be
no motion to his body at all as he fled from the field. He was
one of the smoothest-running two-year-old horses ever seen
and he had no trouble getting there first and taking down first
money of $91,000.

In a little more than 35 minutes on the clock, Mr. Fitz had
earned $17,800 for himself. With these kind of horses and
purses, he has earned anywhere from $50,000 to $125,000 a
year during the last thirty years. Now any time a person pulls
in money of this sort you are going to see it or hear about it.
It will come in the form of a new Cadillac or it will come with
head-shaking and grimaces during a conversation about
how much taxes have to be paid. But you are going to know
the guy you are with makes money.

Mr. Fitz has a different way of handling this. "Money's all
right if you have it," he says, "but I don't see where it means
so much as long as you have enough to live on. There's things
a lot more important."

He was telling this to a person who has spent much of his
life playing tag with the gas company, several barkeepers, a
bookmaker or two, and the mortgage department of a bank.
Coming from anyplace else, this financial advice would have
been regarded as nothing more than platitudes. But when this
simple, bent-over, little old man talks to you somehow it
makes sense. Who needs a thousand dollars' worth of carpeting,
you figure, as long as he has a wife, kids in good health, and
the inevitable clean set of underwear each day.

It is Mr. Fitz's way and, if you were to be Mr. Fitz when he
walks into Barn 17 at Belmont Park each day and see him,
with his vests hanging to his knees and his age and his stoop
from arthritis, you would know that his way gives him something precious.

There was a morning last fall when Chico, one of the grooms,
was leading a filly named Oil Slick around the soft dirt of the
barn's shedrow and the horse was bothering him.

"Boss," he called to Mr. Fitz. "You take a look here. She walk no good. The right front foot. She keep leemping on it."

Mr. Fitz came up to the horse, then curled himself up into a little bundle and bent down. He put his two strong-looking hands on the horse's thin ankle. The filly put her head down as Mr. Fitz touched the leg, but he started to talk to her softly. "Come on now, nice little filly, pick it up. I ain't going to hurt you. Come on, nice little filly. Lift it up. I want to help you."

He kept pushing the leg and the horse finally picked it up and bent it and Mr. Fitz started to run his fingers over the ankle.

"Little fillin' right here, Chico," he said. "See where it is? It's not too bad. Shouldn't be hurtin' her all that." Then he let go of the leg and stood up again. "Leg paint and a wet bandage," he said. "Don't walk her no more today. Heat should go out of it in a day or so and she'll be all right then."

Then he walked away toward his car, which was parked outside the barn entrance. "That one's a Royal Charger filly," he was saying. "She's only a two-year-old. I don't know much about how good she's going to do yet. It takes a long time to find out if you're going to have a horse who can make it. You just got to be there with them every day and keep workin' and maybe someday she'll come around and start doin' what we got her here for."

Mr. Fitz got behind the driving wheel of the car. "If you're afraid of drivin' with me you better get out now and walk," he said. "Lot of fellas don't like driving with me." He started the car and, looking through the steering wheel for vision, drove past a couple of stables and down a block to a small parking space alongside the track's rail. He got out and climbed up the steps to a small tower which is used by trainers to watch their horses in the morning.

A race track at this hour is one of the few places where you can forget everything. In the afternoon, the place becomes crowded and people make noise, and money is the big

53

thing. But in the morning a race track gleams from dew and sunlight and the track is alive with horses. They pass by in groups of three or four, moving at a gallop with exercise boys standing in the stirrups and talking or singing to them. Or they come alone, or maybe two of them, side by side, and they come fast, with the boys flat on their stomachs trying to get more speed from the animals under them. The steady clump of hoofs hitting soft dirt and the snorting of the horses moving fast are the loudest sounds you hear. It becomes very important to listen to these sounds and to stand there and look at the horses. Off in the distance you can see a parkway crammed with cars, their drivers heading for Manhattan and a day's work. And every few minutes a commuter train of the Long Island Rail Road rushes into view for a moment. They are, if you look at them, reminders of the worry and bleakness and effort that goes into working for a living. But if you notice this it means you are not doing your job at the track correctly. The task at hand requires a man to listen to the horses as they pass and to look at them very closely. When you do this, the urge becomes strong to forget tomorrow's business appointment, get a couple of old vests like Mr. Fitz wears and come to the track with him forever.

The old man took out a stop watch and Jimmy Fitzsimmons and Al Robertson, a stable foreman, came up to stand alongside him.

"There he is now," Robertson said. He pointed across the track. The running oval at Belmont is a mile and a half around so a horse can be hard to see when he's way over on the other side, but Mr. Fitz, without using glasses, made him out right away.

"He'll break right from that pole," Mr. Fitz said.

"Royal Record," Robertson said.

"Ready," Robertson said. "Okay, here he goes. *Bing!*"

The "*bing!*" means that the horse had started his run. Mr. Fitz's thumb pressed down on his big silver stop watch.

Far across the track, Royal Record took off. The exercise boy was a shifting package of khaki work clothes as the horse reached out into a long, flowing stride. He flew by the white rail posts and, as he hit a furlong post, Robertson said *"bing!"* again and Mr. Fitz thumbed the stop watch.

"Thirteen," Robertson said.

Mr. Fitz was looking at the watch. "Uh huh," he said.

Now Royal Record seemed to be picking up more and at the next *"bing!"* it was 25 2/5 and at the third it was 37 2/5. Then the boy stood up and started to slow him down to a gallop midway through the stretch, but Royal Record was shaking his head and trying to fight the boy so he could keep going. When they passed the tower Mr. Fitz called out to the exercise boy, "Whoa, Tommy, bring him up now," and when the boy had the horse settled Mr. Fitz left the stand and went back to his car.

Back in the cottage across from the barn Mr. Fitz sat down at the kitchen table, tucked an old piece of plaid cloth, once part of a horse blanket, into place as a bib and had a bowl of vegetable soup.

"That's a two-year-old," he was saying. "Horse hasn't won yet. Had him in a couple of times, but we can't tell much yet. You got to give him time. Young horse. That's this business. I got to keep workin' 'em and givin' 'em time, son."

In the third race at Aqueduct that Saturday afternoon, Royal Record started to come along. He broke well, then picked up the leaders on the turn and, with the crowd in the huge cement and steel stands roaring, Royal Record slammed down the stretch a length and a half to the good and never let anything catch him.

Mr. Fitz sat on a bar stool in a little space in front of the winner's circle that the Pinkerton guards keep clear for him. He grunted a little as Royal Record began to pull away far up the stretch. His face showed no expression as the horse pounded past at the finish line. When they brought Royal

Record back to the winner's circle, Mr. Fitz got up and peered at the horse's legs. "Come out of it all right," he said quietly. "That's the big thing."

A few races later, Mr. Fitz walked out to the parking lot and John Fitzsimmons got behind the wheel and drove him home. As the car pulled in front of the house two little girls who were playing in front of the house next door ran over and each of them kissed the old man as he got out of the car. Then they ran back to their game.

"Belong to the neighbors," he said. "Nice kids. Plenty of pep to 'em."

Then he went inside and flicked on the television set. He is a great television watcher and weekend visitors should be prepared for a session of watching Lawrence Welk or several of those Sunday afternoon "arguin' programs," which is what he calls panel shows. This time Mr. Fitz put on a perfectly wonderful shoot-'em-up and while the Indians made one helluva run at the stage, Mr. Fitz commented on their mounts.

"That gray horse at the back there," he said. "He should catch all those others. He's got the best runnin' action. Of course you can't tell with these things. Somebody's likely to shoot him and he'll be out of the money."

"Can you tell anything about Royal Record after today?"

"Nonsense," he snorted. "I can't tell anything more about him right now than anybody else. Except he won a race today. He's just learnin' now. Next year we'll find out maybe. We'll keep at him and then he'll muscle up some more, get a little bigger and stronger, and then see how far he goes next year."

Then he smiled a little bit. "But that's the nice thing about it," he said softly. "You're always lookin' ahead. Don't have time for anything that happened yesterday. That's gone. What's ahead is what's important. Makes livin' nice."

If you said that, because of a young horse like Royal Record, Mr. Fitz had, at eighty-seven, a reason to live for the future, he would gag and snort. That's too fancy a statement for his tastes. But if you said that he would have to get up at a little after five o'clock in the morning to take care of the horse he would agree. That's his style. Simple and beautiful.

4. The Business

The shedrow was shaded and cool, and up in the rafters a
family of sparrows darted back and forth and talked to each
other. An old dog, part Dalmatian, mainly lazy, stretched out
on the soft dirt and went to sleep. This was at Mr. Fitz's Barn
17 at Belmont Park late one afternoon, but it could have been
at Hialeah or Fort Erie or Gloucester or any of the other tracks
he has been on during his life because stables, and the people
in them, never seem to change. There were twenty-six horses
in the barn on this day, but only one of them, a dark bay, had
his head sticking out of the stall. He was tugging at the bundle
of hay and timothy hanging from in front of the stall. Mr. Fitz
was sitting on a camp chair in the middle of the barn, looking
out into the back where stablehands were busy taking care of
a filly named Leix, who had just been brought back to the
stable after winning a mile-and-three-eighths race that was a
demanding, never-let-up contest every step of the way. There
were four grooms around her. Three of them kept squeezing
big sponges of water over Leix's back and the horse gleamed
like plate glass as the bright sunlight struck her wet back. The
fourth groom held a big tub of water which Leix was drinking
from. The chain on her halter kept rattling against the tub as
she swallowed. When the grooms started to rub a liniment

onto Leix, the horse didn't twitch a muscle. She stood there as if she expected this kind of treatment.

"Good-looking animals, aren't they?"

"They ain't in a beauty contest, son," the old man said.

Which they are not. Thoroughbred race horses are the athletes of the animals. They are high-strung and fragile and their business is speed, the kind of body-wrecking speed which calls for every bit of blood and courage their hearts can pump. The horses, and their speed, are Mr. Fitz's way of life. He sees these animals as people who have a rare ability, but who must be cared for constantly or they will have no chance to show it at all. With Mr. Fitz, racing is a business that calls for you to take a horse and nurse him along and teach him the best way to do the thing for which he was bred and born—run, and never stop running and put so much into it that even a broken leg won't stop the process.

To an awful lot of people, racing is a business of winning or losing, of tote boards and handicapping and money. The sport tells its story to them in the five-point agate type of result charts in newspapers or in stories filled with figures about the amount of money bet or the value of a big stakes race on Saturday. Running race horses before the public has come to mean, in these times, nothing more than a crap game with dice that have four legs.

It is different with Mr. Fitz. He has won in racing, and won as few ever have in any endeavor. But the more you are with him, the further away the business of winning or losing seems to get. And the animals become people and the fascination of tinkering with them is all that really seems to count. Get them to try to do their best. Get everybody around them to do the same thing. The result, win, lose or draw, is something that just happens. The effort is so much more important. It is his way, and it is something you have to know about if you are going to understand this man as he is.

After working with horses for all these years, Mr. Fitz has come to the conclusion that a horse is not any dumber, pro-

portionately, nor burdened with any more poor personal qual-
ities, than humans. In fact he has always felt that a horse
gives more of himself in nearly every circumstance than do
humans. This makes it rather hard to be a full-blooded Fitzsimmons because the old man constantly measures you
alongside the performances given by his horses.

There was, for example, the afternoon several years ago at
the Saratoga race track when Mr. Fitz was standing in the
infield with grandson Jimmy while one of his horses, Cleve,
came around the final turn well behind the pack. Cleve was
a horse born a trifle slow and this unfortunate condition did
not change. But he was still straining with all-out strides as
he came around the turn and the sight of him doing this,
while a good 15 lengths off the lead, caused grandson Jimmy
to laugh.

"Look at Cleve," he said to the old man. "Running himself
right into the ground. He couldn't catch those horses if he
had help."

Mr. Fitz didn't take his eyes off Cleve. "Let me tell you
something," he grunted. "That horse that you're makin' fun of
is tryin' the best he can. Now if you go all through life and
you try to do things right as hard as this horse is tryin' right
now; if you do that, son, then you're going to be quite a man."

Mr. Fitz left the track later that day and when somebody
asked him how Cleve ran, he told them, "Fine. Did the best
he could. Can't ask more than that."

Doing the best you can is a law of his life. You see this all
the time. One night last winter, during the Hialeah racing
season, Mr. Fitz was in the living room in the little house he
keeps on Northwest 42nd Street in Miami, watching a television rerun of a $25,000 race in which one of his fillies, War-
like, had finished well up the track earlier in the day.

"We'll get another look at this," he was saying. "No, I don't
like watchin' us lose another race. But I want to see somethin'
again."

On the screen, Warlike was running a strong second going

down the backstretch. Halfway around the final turn she slipped to fourth, but was still in the running. Then at the head of the stretch, with a horse named Indian Maid leading, a Calumet Farm horse called Teacation came on the outside of Warlike, ran with her, then pulled away and made a run at the leader. Warlike stopped badly.

"That's where she got into trouble," Mr. Fitz said. "That Calumet horse kept her packed in behind them other horses. The dirt got into her face. Horses in front of her kicked it up square into her face. She don't like it none at all. If she was on the outside there, away from it, she'd of been all right. But the Calumet horse kept her tied in there."

"Didn't look as if she ran into that much dirt," Allie Robertson said.

"She got enough to bother her," Mr. Fitz said. "That's what's been holdin' her down. She's got to get over thinking that dirt is so bad. It isn't going to hurt her none. We have to break her of that habit." Mercifully, he turned the television off after the race faded out. "Could she have won the race without the dirt?" he mused. "Oh, I don't know that. But I do know she could have run better. That's the main thing. If she finished fifth and was doin' her best, then we got no complaints. But she finished fifth or sixth or whatever it was and she wasn't doin' her best. That's the big thing. You got to do the best you can with what you got, son."

Mr. Fitz conducts his life under this philosophy while surrounded by the biggest uproar of money, gambling, color, and noise a sport in this country has produced. To an awful lot of people, Mr. Fitz's horse, as he fits into modern racing, is either one or two things. If the horse runs a bit slow, he is a reminder that six per cent interest, as compounded by finance companies, does more to break a man than a depression. And if the horse runs fast enough to win, he is a pretty sight, but one not to waste time on as long as a cashier's window is nearby. This is anything but the attitude of a few. In recent years racing's size has become awesome. Each year now, something like 45,000,000 people bet about $3,250,000,000 at race tracks. There are twenty-five states in which the sport is legal and they cheerfully get into the act. Last year they took $243,388,655 in taxes from racing and politicians have grown to love it. In New York, Governor Nelson Rockefeller said one day, "I am, of course, against gambling on moral grounds." However, the governor was, a month later, conspicuous at the opening of a big new track, Aqueduct, and he made many references to the annual ninety million or so his state receives in revenues from racing.

This side of racing, the side where it is strictly gambling, is a world away from Mr. Fitz. You could see that one fall afternoon at Belmont Park in 1957. Between races he sits on a small wooden bench alongside the enclosure where the horses are saddled, and on this day he was happily ensconced on his bench a short while after the Futurity, a rich and historic race, had been run. The winner was a horse called Jester, owned by George D. Widener. Misty Flight, trained by Mr. Fitz, ran second. But a claim of foul had been lodged against the winner by a horse which had finished fourth. The jockey on that one said Jester had veered over and interfered with him. If the foul claim were allowed by stewards, Mr. Fitz's horse would be listed as the winner and the many people standing around him holding winning tickets on Misty Flight would be in business. And Mr. Fitz would be the winner of a $90,000 stakes race.

"I hope they don't allow it," Mr. Fitz said. "Nothin' bothered my horse. He run it fair and square and got beat. No, I don't want to win like that. I'll take second and stick with it. The horse is all right. He give it a good try. I don't want any more than that."

A few minutes later, the tote board said the result was official; Jester was the winner. The foul claim had been disallowed.

"That's good," Mr. Fitz said. Then he looked at the people around him, who were busy ripping up tickets on Misty Flight.

"Serves you right, hangin' around here and bettin' like fools,"
he said.

His life with these strange, beautiful animals shows he has
this attitude. "All those winners," he was saying one day,
"could've lost just as easy. Then where would we be today?"

He was in the kitchen of his Belmont Park cottage and son
John walked in from the next room with a piece of writing
tablet paper, on which was penciled the record of a horse
called Agnes D.

"This was an important horse to Pop," John said. "This is the
first horse he trained that won a race at a major race track.
Take a look at it. You'll see why we don't get cocky around
here."

On April 30, 1903, the paper said, Agnes D, ridden and
trained by James E. Fitzsimmons, finished sixth in a race at
Jamaica. Then with a change of jockeys, Agnes D won at
Morris Park on May 24. So on June 4, Trainer Fitzsimmons
invaded the big time—Brooklyn's Gravesend track. Agnes D
went to the post, but was acting up and the assistant starter
took a good hold. Too good. The field went away with Agnes
D calmly standing at the post, the assistant starter holding her
tightly. The next time out, June 11, the horse broke fine and
got home first. It was a big day for Mr. Fitz.

"But you see," John Fitzsimmons said, "she learned a new
trick in that first race at Gravesend. It's hard enough to get a
horse into good habits, much less start teaching her bad ones."

On the next time out, July 8, Agnes D remembered standing
at the post and watching the field go. Worse, she had fond
memories of it. When the field broke, she didn't twitch a muscle. And, despite all tutoring, she kept up a pattern in
races, from then on, that was murder. It went like this: July
17, Brighton Beach, Left at Post; July 30, Jamaica, Win; August 14, Saratoga, Win; September 2, Coney Island, Left at
Post; September 21, Gravesend, Left at Post.

"Habits," Mr. Fitz said. "Once they get to doin' things, you got trouble. They can show you that you're not so smart. Do it in a hurry, too."

"Gallant Fox, Pop," John said.

"Oh, yes, well I don't think that was exactly trouble but it goes to show you that they know what's going on, don't worry about that. Well, back in 1930 Gallant Fox was the best horse we had around here. I guess he was the best horse anybody else had around, too, because he won the Kentucky Derby and the Preakness and the Belmont. Won all them big three-year-old races. Well, this one knew where things stood in a race. Anytime he was really goin' for it and there were horses in front of him, he'd have his ears flat back on his head. But the minute he'd pass horses and get out there on the lead and he'd figure he had it won, Pop! Up come the ears. They'd be standing straight up, like he was tryin' to hear something. Why out here in the Lawrence Realization he had a kind of a tough time with a horse called Questionnaire. He was runnin' behind most of the way. Then Sande, yes, that's Earl Sande, he was doin' the ridin', well Sande gets him to move and now it turns into a close thing. Must be something like seventy yards from home and Gallant Fox gets his nose out in front. Make it a little more than that. Gets half a head out in front. Now he's only a couple of jumps from the wire and anything can happen. But Pop! The ears went straight up, as if he was saying, 'That takes care of that.' It was life and death to win the thing, but he didn't seem worried about it at all."

John had been digging through a pile of old boxes and magazines and now he came back with an eight-by-ten photo of the race's finish. The great Earl Sande had his face buried in Gallant Fox's mane and his big hands were wrapped in the reins. It was a picture of a jockey riding all-out at the wire. Clods of dirt flew from under each horse's hoofs. Gallant Fox had, at best, that half a head on Questionnaire. It was anything but a convincing margin. But the ears were straight up.

"That's what got him into trouble," Mr. Fitz said. "He lost interest when he passed a horse. Lost the Tremont to Whichone because of that. He passed Whichone in the stretch, then just about stopped dead. He was looking around and Whichone come right back and passed him and by the time the Fox got going again it was too late. There was some talk that he was lookin' up at an airplane or something. I don't know about that. All I know is that he lost. But it goes to show you this is no easy business. These aren't mechanical rabbits. They're nice animals, all right. Pretty. But they take an awful lot of care and they can get in trouble a lot of ways. You can go to bed at night with a horse worth a million dollars in the barn and when you come around to look at him in the morning he might not be worth a quarter. Gets sick or something and he's not worth anything. It happens all the time. And when you get them to a race they're liable to do anything. Even Gallant Fox lost one on me. Goes to show you.

"Your biggest trouble is with the legs, of course," he went on. "You've seen how thin they are. Well, son, when a horse runs all his weight comes down on one leg. His lead leg. Here, I'll show you." Mr. Fitz cupped his hands and held them out in front of him. "Now when a horse runs it goes like this." He began to make motions with his hands. Each hand was supposed to be a front leg of a horse. Mr. Fitz began to make little running motions with them, then he stopped. "No, I'm not doing it right. Here, maybe it's this way." Then he started moving them in another pattern. "No, that isn't it, either." He grunted a little. "Oh, John!" he called. John came into the room again. "Show him how a horse runs," Mr. Fitz snapped.

The first inclination was to look out the window. Obviously, if Mr. Fitz couldn't illustrate the basic moves of an animal he has lived with and worked with for seventy-six years, age finally has taken an awful lot out of him.

But as John brought in a book which was opened to a series of drawings of the thoroughbred in motion, Mr. Fitz wanted to make sure this idea was not kept in mind.

"Pay attention to it now," Mr. Fitz barked. Then his eyes flashed. "Let me tell you something, son. Maybe I can't show

66

you how they run right here. But you put a horse out on that track and get him to steppin' along pretty good and I'll tell you whether he's doin' it right or not. They don't give me any time to learn how to draw pictures. I'm too busy out there gettin' them to do it the right way."

Then for the rest of the afternoon, Mr. Fitz and John sat in this quiet little cottage and talked about what it is like to train horses that race. And as they talked, Belmont's huge stands, just beyond the stable area gate, filled with people and smoke from their cigarettes and cigars caused a blue haze to hang in the air. There was a big roar when the first race got off. The stands, with their noise and money, were only a short walk from Mr. Fitz's cottage. But they were really so far away that you could never measure it. For as Fitzsimmons spoke of horses you saw how silly it was to regard them as good bets or bad bets or anything else. They are, instead, people that require so much from those around them that, if you do the job right, the way Mr. Fitz does, it leaves you very little time in which to attend to such personal matters as getting old.

"The horse," John explained, "is ancient. Centuries ago, he was only eighteen inches high. He had three toes, but over the years two of them kind of got sloughed off and all that's left of them now are little splint bones, as we call them. Now their upper leg is the same as our lower arm. But what's under that upper leg is where all the trouble comes from. You see, the leg is awfully thin. And in the running motion of a horse, he pushes off with his hind legs and lands on one front leg. We call that the lead leg. Most horses lead with the left leg. So with each stride you have one leg coming down onto the ground with a thousand pounds of weight on it. That's where all the injuries come from."

"The nerves are fine," Mr. Fitz said, "but the blood doesn't circulate too good down there. So if something happens, a good bump will do it as well as anything else, it takes a long time to heal. The blood doesn't move fast enough to help the healing along. They get hurt so easy it scares you. Every morning, when I put horses out there on the training track, I'm worried until they're finished and I see them all back in the barn. The minute one of my horses puts a foot on a race track, even if it's just for an easy gallop, I'm takin' chances with him."

Mr. Fitz usually has to worry about a horse for three years. He gets his first look at a new horse in early January at Hialeah Park. All thoroughbred horses have a universal birthday, January 1, so he is a two-year-old when he is unloaded from a van and walked into the Fitzsimmons barn for the first time. As a two-year-old, the horse is schooled, then run in the shorter races for horses of that age. At three, the objective is to get him to the glamour races, the Kentucky Derby, Preakness, Belmont Stakes, and the like. But the odds are tremendous against this—the average Derby field of about sixteen is the best that can be mustered from an original crop of some eight thousand thoroughbreds foaled in Kentucky, Maryland, Virginia, California, and Florida three years before. Usually, you have to settle for a lot less than the big races. Then, as a four-year-old the horse is in races where the distances get longer, the amount of weight placed on his back becomes heavier and the competition is tougher. There is a big difference in ability between a two- and three-year-old and a three- and four-year-old. A two-year-old is like a boy in grammar school. A horse at three is the same as a high school kid. After that you get to the varsity.

The main job, if you are training a horse, is to find out what is 100 per cent of his ability. In the beginning, races will not, as a rule, show it to you. Dirt in the face, a poor start, sulking under a whip, a bad ride by the jockey, things like these will obscure his basic ability. The only place to start finding out is in the morning. The only standard you can use is time. You run a horse against a clock, then watch him closely when he gets back from the workout. By the time the exercise boy pulls up the horse and brings him back to where the trainer is standing, the horse should be breathing normally. If he is in distress, his sides heaving as he gasps for breath, then he has been worked too fast. By trial and error against the clock you come up with a picture of the horse's true ability. After that, the job is to get it out of him. Which is where all the work comes in. In life, somebody may be a drunk or beat his wife or be dead lazy and never get anyplace. On a race track, a horse might be too curious and not pay attention to business or he might be too nervous. Or he might not like to have another horse come alongside and test him, stride for stride, and he'll quit, the same as an awful lot of humans give up if you look them in the eye and ask them for the best they've got.

To do it properly, training horses is a long, tedious job and you've got to know these animals and actually have a love for them to do it right. This does not mean you fling your arms around a horse and nuzzle him at every opportunity. The most you'll get out of this is a decent-sized bite on the shoulder. But there must be a basic liking for the horse or the job never will get done. Mr. Fitz, for example, shows little emotion as he stomps around the barn each morning. "I'm just here to wreck these horses by makin' 'em work hard," he says. But one morning, when he had his horses quartered at the old Aqueduct track, he was leaning against a barn talking to a couple of people who had come around to take pictures of horses so they could gag the neighborhood with some home movies at later dates.

"You want to see my horses?" Mr. Fitz said. His eyes lit up a little. "Why, that's wonderful. Now you stay right here with me." Then he called out to one of his foremen, "Get Nashua out here." The man went into the barn and he came out leading Nashua, a huge, strapping animal who held his head proudly and looked around. Nashua did a gentle little dance as the stablehand held him. The visitors beamed and began to talk about how beautiful the horse was. This was right up Mr. Fitz's alley. "Get Bold Ruler out here, too," he called and a kid said yes he would and he came out of the stable holding the Ruler. "Put 'em right together so these people can look at them," the old man said.

They put Nashua, who was four, and Bold Ruler, who was two and much lighter and sleeker, side by side and as the people clucked over them, the old man smiled. "Nice horses," he kept saying. "Real nice horses. They're nice to work with. No, these aren't my favorites. I don't have any favorite horses. It's just like havin' a family. The ones who can't keep up and need some help you worry the most about. Now I got some horses in the barn there that are a little weak and need some extra attention. They're the ones you got to try and help along."

This bit of sentiment disposed of, Mr. Fitz stamped his crutch on the ground. "All right, take 'em back," he called. "I don't have time to stand around here admirin' 'em. I've got to get to work with the rest of 'em around here. They're not going to like it much because I'm goin' to put 'em through their paces the best I can.

"I don't know whether the horse knows me or not," Mr. Fitz says. "If you come around here with sugar and give it to 'em two, three days in a row they'd want to know you a damn sight better than they know me. Oh, I guess they know my voice. They don't like it much, either. They hear me they know it means hard work. When they hear somebody else comin' around clucking to 'em and with a pocket full of sugar lumps they're a lot happier. It's just like the teacher in school. I don't think kids like to hear her comin' along with a whole lot of work in her hands. They'd rather have the candy store man pattin' 'em on the head and reachin' for some sweets. But the teacher is a lot more important. At least I hope she is. Because that's what I'm doin' with these horses. Teachin' 'em to mind their business and do things right. And they know a lot more than you think they do.

"You take Nashua. Allie Robertson was always with that horse, washin' him down, pattin' him. Well, when Nashua was sent down to the farm in Kentucky, Leslie Combs' place in Lexington, they use Nashua for breedin' down there, you

70

know, well, anyway, Nashua is down there for over a year
when Allie happened to get down there. He had to ship there
with another horse. Allie says he went lookin' for Nashua
and he saw the horse out in a paddock chewin' some grass and
loafin' along. Allie got behind a tree and he says, 'Hey, Mickey!
Mickey!' We used to call the horse Mickey around the barn.
Well, the minute Nashua hears that he starts to go wild.
Started running all over the place. He knew that voice all
right. And he began lookin' for it, too. So I guess horses can
get to know you, all right. But it's more important for me to
know the horses. You'll never do any good in this business unless you understand every little habit a horse has. You've got
to be able to stand out there in the morning and look at the
horse and have some sort of an idea whether he's all right or
not.

"Sometimes you can tell how a horse feels by the way he's
standing. If you look at him enough and get to know that he
likes to stand in the front of the stall and look out, then you
come around and find him in the back with his head sticking
into a corner, then it could mean something's the matter with
him. You've got to look at the horse a lot to know this. Every
chance you get, look him over. Study everything he does. Then
if you get to know him as well as you should you can tell if
something's been botherin' him. Then you can take care of it.
If you don't notice something wrong and you put the horse
out onto the track and run him, he's liable to fall apart. Lord
knows they fall apart easily enough without somebody makin'
a mistake and hurrying it along. It takes a lot of looking. You've
got to do it all the time."

This looking, if you are around Mr. Fitz in the mornings,
seems to be a casual thing. After his horses are worked—they
are sent out onto the track in groups of five or six; "sets" in
race track terms—they are brought back to circular enclosures
of grass behind the barn. Stableboys then walk them in a
circle—"hot-walking"—for about 45 minutes to allow the horse
to cool off gradually. While they're doing this, Mr. Fitz sits in

71

a chair and watches them. To a visitor, it looks like he's loafing. But if you sit beside him and start to promote a conversation, you are not going to get far.

"Now I'd like to sit here and talk to you all day," he explained one morning, "but you're gettin' in the way of my job. I've got to watch these horses. Watch every step they take. And think about 'em. And if you're going to sit here and talk about some nonsense that happened last night I'm not going to get very far."

An unfortunate thing about his job as Mr. Fitz sees it, is that the final result must always be in the hands of a jockey. He is an old jockey himself, but has never seemed to be in any particular ecstasy over the little men who climb on his horses and ride them for money in the afternoon. As a rule, in the stories about racing that you read about in newspapers and magazines, the jockey is the big thing. If Willie Shoemaker or Eddie Arcaro ride a couple of winners in a day they automatically rate headlines. And in the stands—the "betting ring," as the old man calls it—the experts do much of their figuring with jockeys. As many people as not do their betting on the strength of the jockey riding a particular horse. If an Arcaro or a Shoemaker is up, a horse which should be a legitimate 5–1 or more in the betting, goes off at 4–1 or less because of this.

"You take all the time we spend takin' care of a horse," Mr. Fitz says. "It adds up to a lot of work. We get to know everything we can about the animal. Now when it's time to run him in a race, it seems the jockey becomes the important one. There's so much talk about jockeys that sometimes I wonder if we're havin' jockey races instead of horse races."

Mr. Fitz has some comments on horsemanship in general. "Take whipping, for example. There's no need to whip a horse as a rule. Most horses get out there and try their best. So if you hit him it isn't going to do anything but hurt. It's just like hollerin' at somebody who's doin' his best. It's discouraging. When you've got a horse out there trying, the rider should try to help him. Hold his head up and sort of keep him together. But these fellas get nervous and start hitting with the whip. It does no good at all. Another thing I don't like about them is the way they ride short. The stirrups are so short all they can do is kind of fold their legs up and just hang on and ride. There's no way to really direct the horse. They don't have that much leverage.

"When I rode, we rode long. The stirrups were down further and you had a chance to use your legs to direct the horse. Not today. Oh, they do one thing better than we did. When I rode, we'd sit up kind of straight in the saddle. These boys are down, with their head lower than the horse's. That kind of cuts down the amount of wind they buck. It helps 'em go a little faster, I guess. And they all get as far forward on the horse as they can. Which is the right way. But there's other things I don't like. You take a young horse, a two-year-old. Well, the minute one of these boys breaks him from the gate during a race they'll get out there a little bit and the first thing they do is, whoa! They start taking him back. Pulling him in. It gets kind of tight out front there and they want to come back and get a little room. It's a lot safer that way. But what about the horse? They're teaching him a bad habit. Hell, I don't want the horse to stop. He's going, then keep him going. But they'll pull him back every time. Pretty soon the horse goes out there and stops on his own.

"These boys have no reason to do it. If they're afraid, they have no business riding. You'll never find Arcaro doing that. Oh, not him. If the horse wants to run, he'll go with it. He takes a chance every time. You're not going to find him backing off. No, sir. Eddie gets a horse right out there for you, whether it's crowded or not. And he does it every day, too. Not just once in a while when there's big money around. Put him on a horse in any race and he'll give you the best he can. And he'll let the horse do the best he can, too. That's what we're all here for, son."

Mr. Fitz got up and walked out of the house and across the

road to the barn to tell Jasper, one of his foremen, about something he wanted done with the horses. Barn 17 had that usual ammonia-hay smell, strong enough to bring an alcoholic back to life. It is a smell that you find nowhere else except at a clean horse barn. Because of this, it is anything but a bad smell. Early in the morning, after a night of being a bad boy, it makes the legs stiffen and the eyes burn. But even then it isn't bad. As Mr. Fitz walked into the barn and started to talk, curious heads began to stick out from each stall. Aside from a few shakes of the head to shoo a fly away, the heads looked at the bent-over old man and nothing else. It was a wonderful place to spend an afternoon. It is the only side of racing Mr. Fitz cares about. "Nice life," he said quietly.

5. The Green Years

The place was called The Lamp and it was across the street from the docks where the charter fishing boats leave Sheepshead Bay every morning. The juke box was playing something by Glenn Miller, saxophone over clarinet, the way it used to be in the late 1930s, and then the music changed and Bunny Berigan was playing "I Can't Get Started with You" which is of the same years. Berigan must have been a genius. He made music while the whiskey was making his legs stagger and his fingers stiff, yet here it was, still good enough to be coming out of a box and into a place in Sheepshead Bay in 1961.

The girl who was at the bar with her boy friend didn't like it at all. "Unh," she said to her boy friend. "Where do you get all this old stuff from? I don't like nothing old like this. We might as well be in a museum, you sit listening to old stuff like this."

She was about twenty and she probably had a good complaint. Things from the past can seem fine if you have been there yourself. But it is different if you have not. Then when somebody starts saying about how he could get a five-cent glass of beer in his time somebody who was not there is going to ask him how many kids used to die from diphtheria in those days because they hadn't found a vaccine for it. It is always hard to understand about the past. You've got to sit down and make yourself imagine what it was like.

You could see this a couple of minutes later when the guy who owned The Lamp walked across the room and tapped his hand on a big Currier & Ives print he had hanging on the wall over the booth.

"This was a great big race," he said.

The print was of a horse called Proctor Knott, his nostrils wide open as he sucked in air, defeating Salvator in the Futurity of 1888 at Sheepshead Bay race track.

"The First Futurity," the owner said. "They run it right up the block here. The track was off Ocean Avenue. You look at all the apartment houses they got there now, you'd never know it. But they had a big race track there." He looked up at the picture. "These days here, it's like they're from another world. You know what I mean?"

Yes. The picture was of a horse race, but it was a race out of the era that produced Sunny Jim Fitzsimmons. And you have to go into them and understand them, even if they were a long time ago, if you want to understand his career. Although he is alert and active and a winner here in 1961, everything Mr. Fitz does, all his opinions and outlooks and habits, they all started at a time that only a very few today are alive to remember.

Late one afternoon in the fall of 1877, T. R. Jackson, a successful New York architect, walked into his office on lower Broadway after a long lunch uptown at Delmonico's. Luncheon included a ton of rye and water and Jackson felt great. More important, stuffed in his jacket pocket was a commission from Pierre Lorillard, William K. Vanderbilt, and August Belmont, to design a new race track. Now Jackson didn't know much about racing, but that didn't matter to him at all. He knew that Lorillard had a barrel of money from the tobacco business and the names of Vanderbilt and Belmont spoke for themselves. If they wanted a race track, Jackson told his staff, they were going to get just about the best race track anybody ever saw.

The place was to be called the Coney Island Jockey Club and it was to be put up, for the immense sum of $80,000, on a tract of land in the Sheepshead Bay section of Brooklyn. When the land was surveyed and mapped, Jackson got out his T square and compass and a handful of sharp pencils and went to work. He took his time. He was not about to give his big money clients a couple of freehand sketches.

There were a few houses on the land, and when Jackson was finished drawing up his plans he told his clients that the houses had to be cleared out right away to make room for the construction.

"There is one place that can stay a while," he said. "The way I have it now, the house sits right in the middle of what will be your infield. We won't need anything done there until the landscapers come in right at the end, so the people can stay there a while, if they want to."

The people who lived in the house were George and Catherine Fitzsimmons and their seven children, including the next to youngest, who was baptized James E. Fitzsimmons and had been born on July 23, 1874.

The Fitzsimmonses had been born in the old country. George Fitzsimmons was brought to this country from County Meath at age two. Catherine Murphy came over in her mother's arms from Cork in the same year. They were part of the wave of Irish who had to pick up and leave their country during one of the potato famines. They filled steerage on anything floating which was headed for New York. When they landed, a large number of immigrants headed out from the crowded city and settled in Sheepshead Bay, which at the time was a little fishing village surrounded by farmlands. The Bay, as people who live there call it, is part of the Gravesend region of Brooklyn, which flanks one side of the mouth of New York harbor. Officially, Gravesend was a part of New York City, but everybody thought of it as a place you traveled to.

When George Fitzsimmons and Catherine Murphy married, they moved into an old frame house on land owned by some rich people they had never heard of, Lorillard or something, and raised a family. The area was known as Irishtown, which in those days was not exactly an endearing name. By the time their son Jimmy Fitz was born, for example, the New York *Times* had just gotten over the custom of running help wanted ads with the title IRISH NEED NOT APPLY placed boldly over many of them.

Jimmy Fitz was three years old when workmen came around and started to knock down other houses in the area and plow the land up. While carpenters started on the framework of a grandstand, a group of men and some plow horses started the painstaking work of building a running strip for thoroughbred horses that completely encircled the Fitzsimmons house. So somewhere before his fifth birthday, Sunny Jim Fitzsimmons was able, for the first time, to go out his front door, walk a few yards, then dig a toe onto a track surface and see what kind of footing there was along the rail. He had, of course, the perfect background to be a carpenter.

Catherine Fitzsimmons was worried at first when workmen and their heavy construction equipment came around to build the track. Under an agreement with the landlord, she could remain in the house for about a year. This was, she worried, a long time for her children to be running around dangerous equipment.

Her concern faded for her next to youngest son, at least, when a man named Jim Claire, who removed the debris from the place with a wagon, began to leave his workhorses in the barn alongside the Fitzsimmons house each night. Jimmy Fitz was given the treat, each night, of getting up on one of the broad-backed animals and riding him into the barn. He became self-appointed groom, jockey, and general water boy for the two horses and there was one night when a workman, watching him ride one of the animals, said to Catherine Fitzsimmons, "Maybe you people ought to stay here. When the races start, your kid will have a field day. If he doesn't get much bigger he might make a jockey for you. He is crazy about these two old horses. If he treats you as good as these horses you're going to have a fine old age."

The Coney Island Jockey Club track was one of three that was being built in the area and when they were finished the place became the thoroughbred racing capital of the nation. With Gravesend, Brighton Beach, and the Sheepshead track operating, the nation's finest horses and richest owners were found there. The New York social and sporting crowd came down from Manhattan and stayed at big, gaudy hotels which lined the waterfront. The Oriental Hotel, a block-long, four-story mass of wooden spires and verandas, was a vacation showplace. It sat on Manhattan Beach, a few blocks from Sheepshead's fishing piers. On an early summer evening, just after the races, a small Negro string orchestra would play tunes in the dining room, which was crowded with actors, politicians, prize fighters, and such as Diamond Jim Brady, James R. Keene, and the rest of the top-crust of the society-sporting set. The side doors and windows of the restaurant would be open and you could hear the music and listen to the people talking and see the waiters popping magnums of champagne. Out on the street there was a line of barouches, phaetons, and other fashionable rigs of the carriage trade. The drivers sat quietly, smoking, while they waited for their people to finish dinner and call for the drive back to New York, a long one, or the shorter and more picturesque canter along the waterfront to any of the other rambling, gracious hotels which were set back from the beach.

You can understand this kind of living. But for Jimmy Fitzsimmons who lived in Irishtown and moved to another house when the race track was built, it was all different. And it was a kind of life that a kid today never will know about.

Life started in a hurry for anybody growing up in Irishtown. When you were able to walk, you were able to work. When Jimmy Fitz was six years old he was working to help his family

79

have enough food on the table. His father had a huckster
wagon and summer mornings at four o'clock he would hitch
horses to it, go into the house and wake up his son, put him in
the back of the wagon, and then let him go to sleep again
while he would drive to the Wallabout Market in Greenpoint
to get his supplies for the day. It was a drive of an hour and
when he'd get to the market, George Fitzsimmons would wake
his son and have him mind the horses while he went and did
some buying. On the way back, Jimmy Fitz would drive the
horses and his father would sleep. It would be morning, time
to get out and start selling, by the time they got back to
Sheepshead Bay. It would be three or four in the afternoon
before they were through selling the produce. This was the
way Jimmy Fitz started out in the world—with an 11-hour
working day. He never did many of the things you are used to
seeing children doing in the back yard or in a playground because when you are six your body is not very strong and
working 11 hours a day leaves it too tired for play.

Sometimes, it took longer than scheduled to complete a day
because somebody at the market always had a bottle of
whiskey to accustom his body to the pre-dawn air and George
Fitzsimmons was not one to be unsociable. And when a man
takes a drink he just can't up and leave right away.

There was one morning when George Fitzsimmons got the
wagon loaded and was about to climb aboard when he seemed
to remember something.

"You wait right here for a minute," he told his son. "I've got
to go back and see somebody about something."

It wasn't five o'clock yet and there was a good chill in the
air. There wasn't a man in the market who didn't want to see
somebody about something this morning. Two hours later,
George Fitzsimmons came back to the wagon, his face a little
bit red, and his eyebrows bunched up as he tried to put together a good story. He saw his son asleep. He also saw the
way to his alibi.

"Where've you been?" he roared at Jimmy. "You moved this

wagon. We were down two blocks from here when I left. I've been lookin' all over for you."

Then he climbed onto the back of the wagon and fell asleep. Jimmy Fitz drove home and kept trying to remember when the horses had taken off on their own. He decided it must have been when he was asleep, although he could have sworn he was at the same street corner when he woke up. But he didn't argue. It's never a good policy to knock the other guy's story, particularly when he is your father.

Potato farms were an important part of the Sheepshead Bay economy. During the picking season Jimmy Fitz would move with his father out to a neighboring farm. He'd get up at 3:45 in the morning and start to work right away, because the potatoes had to be ready to load on a truck headed for the market at a little after 11 A.M. So George Fitzsimmons would be stooped down, digging the potatoes, and this little kid with him would shake the potatoes off the vine and put them into a basket. At night, Jimmy Fitz would climb up a ladder to a small attic room where they had a pillow and floorboards for him to sleep on. A window had been cut into the room because the garret soaked in the sun each day and retained its worst heat over the night. But the window had no screen over it and mosquitoes came whining in all night, biting the kid and waking him up.

You would make the newspapers if you were found doing this with a boy of six today. But at this time it was common and necessary. There was no question of cruelty or even harshness on children. It was something everybody did and the kids grew up as they always do and nobody thought anything of it.

If it seems hard for somebody today to understand this sort of life, Mr. Fitz has a simple answer. "If you can't imagine it," he was saying one day, "I'll help you. Do you have a kid that's six? Then send him out to work in the fields every day. That'll give you an idea of what it is like."

There were, he says, two general rules of conduct while he was being brought up and everybody in the area adhered to them. "One was, no matter how bad things were, don't you dare touch something that doesn't belong to you. Why you could hang diamonds out on the washline and they'd be there at night. And people were all the same to us. We had colored families and Italians and Irish and Jewish and it didn't make a bit of difference. You lived with the colored same as you lived alongside the Irish. Now I was supposed to have been brought up in hard times. Well, now I got to wonder how hard they could have been. You go around today and you hear people roastin' the Jews or roastin' the colored or some other nationality and the guy doing it don't know why he doesn't like them. He's just sayin' something. You sit him down and ask him why he don't like the ones he's roastin' and he couldn't give you any sort of a worthwhile answer. Well, we had no distinction where I came from and as far as I'm concerned we have to get back to that again before the world is going to get straightened out. When we learn to live together, then everything'll be all right. There's no trick to it, you know. All you got to do is live with people and forget about what they are. That takes a lot less out of you than going around figuring out reasons why you don't like them. When everybody starts learning that, things'll be better."

Of the six other children in Mr. Fitz's family, two are still alive. His brother Tom, only eighty, can be found almost any morning hot-walking horses, stick straight, a cap on his head, heavy army boots on his feet. He looks like you could send him out to do a day's work anyplace. Mr. Fitz's sister Nora is eighty-nine. She is as clear as a bell, lives in Sheepshead Bay and stays up too late watching television at night. The three brothers and a sister who passed away lived to a bit better than average age. Pat, who died in 1955, was eighty. Steve was seventy-five when he died in 1956. Sister Kate died at sixty-seven in 1949 and the oldest in the family, George, was sixty-five when he died in 1932. Apparently, the hard work didn't hurt anybody. Nor did anybody starve. There is always food where there is farmland. All you have to do is work for it. Which is what the Fitzsimmons family did.

School in Sheepshead Bay was a kind of casual thing. At first there was a one-room shack which served as a school. And later a new one was built. But Jimmy Fitz went to school only now and then in the winter and then only when it was too cold to do any working. He didn't learn much of anything, either, but nobody at home was particularly worried about this because food on the table was all that was important. You were not going to get tomorrow's breakfast by sitting in a classroom learning how to do things like reading and writing. Besides, during the spring and fall, when both school and the race tracks operated at the same time, a student in Sheepshead Bay ran a poor second to the scratch sheet with the local schoolmaster. Many afternoons, a few minutes before post time for the first race, the man would clear his throat, mention something about tomorrow morning at nine o'clock, then dismiss the class and run like a thief for the grandstand.

There was time for a few kid things while Jimmy Fitz was growing up, but not a lot. Fist fighting, for one thing, was a lost art with him. He spent so much time working he never did learn how to get away from a left hand. In his only three outings, a boy named George McNulty batted him out each time. In the fighting department, he still is a maiden.

But even with little training, he knew how to maneuver pretty good. When it came to getting a penny for the store or a couple of stray cookies or the other things kids work housewives for, he was a bit faster than the next one. He would go up to somebody's house and announce brightly that the big kids up on the corner had told him to come and run that errand you wanted. When the housewife would say she had no errand in mind, he would put on a little of that sad Irish into his face. The housewife then would do something, either create an errand for the penny or come up with a piece of something, for this poor boy who was fooled by the older ones. This worked out pretty good until he would try it a second time around at each house.

He had one good friend in the Bay. His name was George Tappen, whose father had a small seafood restaurant that later on was to grow into one of New York's best-known eating places. But when Tappen was a boy the place was nothing and he had to do a day's work like any other kid in the Bay. When Jimmy Fitz came to know him well, Tappen had a job minding two horses a man they called Buffalo Bill kept in a paddock behind his saloon. Jimmy Fitz liked to come around and ride the horses bareback. Tappen was attracted to the animals, too. So the two spent afternoons riding the broad-backed horses around the paddock and they kept talking about how much they liked horses, just as they were to talk about these animals for the next seventy years of working together on race tracks.

Aside from working with his father, Jimmy had several types of jobs around the Bay. This was in keeping with the place, for a tradesman in Sheepshead Bay was a man who had to be able to do anything to turn a dollar. There was, for example, Gus Friend, the blacksmith. There were plenty of horses around and usually lots of work to do on them, but he wasn't going to get caught in any financial jackpots if the black-smith business ever became slow. Not Gus. Not while he could be a dentist on the side. Jimmy used to work for him, sweeping out the place, and he liked to hang around and watch the horses being shod. Then one afternoon his sister Nora came in, her hand flattened out on a throbbing jaw. Friend simply nodded, put down his anvil and hammer and, by the simple process of picking up a pair of pliers, became the dentist. Over the years, Friend had earned a reputation for having a light touch with the pliers, so Nora never twitched a muscle while she opened her mouth and pointed to the troublesome tooth. Gus gave it his light-handed yank. It didn't get him anywhere. Another tug or two didn't do much to the tooth, which had come to stay. Mr. Friend put his professional reputation as both a dentist and blacksmith on the line with the next tug. He sent it all in with a yank that would move a dray horse. Nora's tooth came out. So did her jaw. It was dislocated. Nora headed for a doctor, a legitimate one, to get it straightened out.

Mr. Fitz also held a job for a time working for a man named Brunner, who had a provision wagon. Brunner was about his business from dawn to dusk and paid his helper, Mr. Fitz, four dollars a month and meals. He had cheeses, pickle barrels, herring barrels and the like on his horse-drawn cart and hustled his stuff to the people in the area. Jimmy Fitz took orders from the housewives and ran back to the wagon and picked them up. He couldn't read or write at all, but he wanted that four dollars a month, so he developed a system of making little hieroglyphics on a paper bag and he insists he rarely got an order wrong. But dealing with housewives was, of course, murder. Particularly when it came to the herring. They were kept in a cold barrel of brine and to get one you had to reach in the brine up to the elbow. After which, of course, the woman would say it was too small and she wanted a larger one. This could go on for as long as the woman wanted to haggle. This being a woman's first love, he had stiff workouts on the brine barrel.

Brunner, aside from selling whatever he had, continually made small side deals along the route. There was, for example, a Mrs. Van Kutchen, who had money and lived in the elegant Coney Island waterfront section. She kept a goat in her yard which caught Brunner's eye. One afternoon he made a deal with the woman to buy the goat, loaded it on the wagon and started away. Before he left, Mrs. Van Kutchen gave his helper an order for a pound of lamb chops to be delivered the next day. Jimmy Fitz made his little hieroglyphic for chops on the paper bag, then hustled back to the wagon and gave Brunner the order. Brunner took it down carefully. He did not carry lamb chops in his store, but this didn't seem to bother him at all. When Jimmy Fitz started work the next morning, the goat, which he had left tied in Brunner's yard, was not in evidence. And Brunner handed him a package for delivery to Mrs. Van Kutchen. "It's her lamb chops," he said.

Brunner was also murder on the meals. He was a frugal Dutchman who was not going to go for three cents on anything, particularly food for somebody working for him. After awhile, then, his helper began to gag at the thought of another plate of pigs' knuckles and sauerkraut for dinner. For a change of pace, Brunner would throw knockwurst with sauerkraut at him and pretty soon this kind of food knocked Jimmy Fitz out of the box. He made a couple of gentle complaints, but the best he got out of that was heavy on the sauerkraut. He decided to straighten out the deal his own way. He was alone in the storage cellar one afternoon when he spotted a big ham Brunner had ready for the next day's selling. Jimmy Fitz got to work with the knife and had a good-sized piece ready to take home to his mother to cook when Brunner came into the place and caught the move. This was how Jimmy Fitz got his next job cleaning the cesspool for a woman named Callahan who lived on 14th Street.

"I wasn't interested in any of the jobs, anyway," Mr. Fitz says. "All I wanted to do was be around animals. I had jobs minding cows for some women. I minded for three of 'em. Now what I call mindin' cows doesn't mean just standin' there and looking at 'em. I'd have to come and get 'em each morning after they was milked and drive 'em down Ocean Avenue and look for the best grazing land. Then I had to make sure they wouldn't get in anybody's farmland and start eating cabbages and things like that. Then I'd bring 'em back to the woman in time for milkin' late in the afternoon. I had a kind of a goat cart, too. I fixed up an old box with some wheels and I put a harness around the goat. Oh, I was proud of that harness, had it all fixed up nice, and I'd drive the goat all over town. But whatever I did wasn't important except to get money to bring home. All I ever really wanted to do was be with the horses. When they built the tracks and had all them horses around, I wanted to work there. Oh, I was little. Only weighed about 85 pounds or so, but I wasn't thinking too much of being a jockey or anything like that. I just wanted to work with them. Well, one of the jobs I had was delivering milk to the stable kitchens at Sheepshead Bay. You'd bring four, five quarts in a big can to them. When I went there, I was always around there looking at the horses and bothering the people for a job. Tom Healy, he was working for the Walden stable, was one fella I pestered a lot. Then I got to the cook in the kitchen at the Brannan Brothers Stable and one day he said he could use me if I wanted to work and I said yes. That was how I got started in racing."

Jimmy Fitz's start was a strong one. He checked into the Brannan Brothers Stable kitchen at 6:00 A.M. on the morning of March 4, 1885, and got home to his house at dusk with a load on. President Grover Cleveland had been inaugurated in Washington that day and after 14 hours of work at caring for horses, the stable crew threw a small party in honor of the new President. They put together a mess of eggnog and started to work on it when young Jimmy Fitz, as they called him, came out of the kitchen. Somebody handed him a glass of it. Jimmy Fitz tossed down the first drink of his life, did some laughing and then started home. He had to walk through some woods to get over to his house and he found, on this night, the trees getting closer together with each step. The rum from the eggnog was popping in his head now and being an amateur at the business of being stiff he couldn't figure out what was going on. He had to hang onto trees here and there and finally made it home. It was the perfect way to come home from a race track, just about anyplace else you care to name for that matter, but it was the last time he went against whiskey to any extent.

It was the last time he had any time to try it, too. At this time, a race track for a kid working on it was a place where you did your work until it was finished and then you went to bed because there wasn't much time left in the day. The horses were being wintered at Sheepshead Bay—there was no such thing as winter racing in the South as we have today—and without the excitement of afternoon races, the work seemed longer and harder.

"I liked it right off," he says. "Love? Oh, that's one of those strong-sounding words for a thing. But I guess you could call it love. You worked as hard as I did, you had to love animals, I guess."

It is when you start looking into the racing career of Mr. Fitz that you begin to see how old this business of running thoroughbred horses is. The first record of any organized racing, for example, was in 1174 at Smithfield, near London. By the time Mr. Fitz came around, it was a big thing. By comparison, college football had hardly started and professional baseball was just forming. But the races were big. A little too big at times.

Professor J. A. Going was one of the more eminent authorities on horses around. He wrote a column of veterinary advice for horsemen and in it he plugged any of the dozen items he was selling on a mail-order basis at the time. He had a blister ointment which was "prepared on request of prominent horsemen" and which was guaranteed to take care of sprains, splints, and spavins at a cost of 75 cents. For 50 cents Professor Going sold a picture of the anatomy of a horse. In his column, he dealt with such topics as the problem of keeping mice from eating the horse's harness. He had a special solution to rub on the harness to take care of that. Professor Going had competition from the firm of Samuel Garry and Company, 237 Broadway, which put out "Spanule, the Great External Cure. Good for Man and Beast." For man, it was a quick cure for "malarial diseases, wounds, piles, boils, chilblains, bunions, corns." For beasts, it took care of "lameness, sprains, scalds, sores, bruises." It cost 50 cents a pint, a dollar a quart. The Goodwin Brothers of 241 Broadway seemed to be the best mail-order touts of the time, their ads guaranteeing four winners a day. Of course if you had your money up on a particularly hot day for the Goodwin boys, you had way more than that.

Even at this time, racing was a sport that was 215 years old in this country. The first race track in America was established in the spring of 1665 at Salisbury, Long Island, by Colonel Richard Nicolls, a British officer who had taken over the job of running New York when Peter Stuyvesant and the Dutch were forced to surrender the area. Daniel Denton, one of the era's writers, described the place as "toward the middle of Long Island lieth a plain sixteen miles long and four broad, upon which plain grows very fine grass that makes exceeding good hay; where you shall find neither stick or stone to hinder the horse heels or endanger them in races, and once a year, the best horses in the Island are brought hither to try their swiftness, and the swiftest rewarded with a silver cup, two being annually provided for the purpose."

The place was called Newmarket, after the English course, and today it is the site of a public golf course for people who live on Long Island.

After Newmarket was established, there seemed to be all the racing you wanted. Some of it was strictly on the quiet. William Penn, for one thing, had the stallion Tamerlane and two mares on his Philadelphia property in 1699, but rather than offend his fellow Quakers—worse yet, lose their backing—he kept his stock for private use. In Virginia, horsemen were keeping the courts filled with cases involving welshing on bets and such as the pulling of a horse called Smoker, who was lengths the best in a match race with the mare Folly, but was pulled up before the finish line and lost. Chicanery was charged and the matter wound up going to the highest court in the area. As for race tracks as we know them today, Saratoga, opened in 1864 by John Morrissey, an ex-prize fighter, saloonkeeper, and politician, was the first.

But as far as the Coney Island Jockey Club was concerned, everything in racing was amateur night before they put up the Sheepshead Bay Race Track. The "American Ascot," they called it, and they bet at bookmaking booths. Leonard Jerome,

89

whose Jerome Park, in the Bronx, already had fine racing, was named president. His daughter was married and in England. A Churchill, she had named her first son Winston. James Gordon Bennett, the publisher of the New York *Tribune*, put up a $1000 here and there to make the stakes values look a bit better and Pierre Lorillard and James R. Keene were two of the more active members. In 1879, Lorillard didn't even think twice about coming up with $18,000 to buy the great horse Falsetto from J. W. H. Reynolds, another tobacco guy. Falsetto then went on to beat Spendthrift at Saratoga in one of the year's big races. Keene's financial situation was adjudged not to be shaky from the day this goateed ex-prospector and newspaper editor did a little bit of maneuvering with a man named J. P. Morgan and began to play with enough money to buy Russia. Keene also brought a lot of enthusiasm to the game and in his time owned some of the great horses, Sysonby, Peter Pan, and Frizette.

Sheepshead had 430 acres of ground and a rambling, two-decked grandstand. The high-class people who sat in the upper tier box seats found they had a commanding view of the Atlantic, with Sandy Hook jutting out of the water far to the right. The club had promised its best patrons that they would not be molested by the riffraff and lived up to the promise. An upper box at Sheepshead was as good as a seat in the Diamond Horseshoe at the Metropolitan Opera House. Patrons paid 50 cents for general admission, a dollar for clubhouse privileges. They bet at bookmaking booths set up by the firm of James E. Kelly and Joseph Bliss. There were also new machines, imported from France, which sold $5 win tickets. They were called mutuels and were despised by the bookmakers.

Now at this time, people, particularly their legislators, had not grown up enough to understand that there was nothing immoral about gambling. Betting on anything, even at a place owned by such as Pierre Lorillard, was illegal. The thought of enforcing the law, however, was as distant to authorities as having it repealed. It was, at this time, one of those strange little shams this country for some reason always has had.

Yet there were certain formalities which were to be observed and this accounted for the visit, early one May morning, of Mr. James E. Kelly to the office of Chief John Y. McKane, who was in charge of all police in the Gravesend area, was active in politics and became known as the "Czar." He was to get in trouble later in his career, but all anybody in Sheepshead Bay knew about him was that he was a man who would give the poor a break, and this was much more important than anything which came out of a political feud which put McKane into hot water later on.

"Morn'n to you, Chief Kane, and I know you're busy so I won't take much of your time, and would you please close the door?" Kelly said.

Kane said hello. Then he closed the door.

"I can't stand hypocrites," Kane said. "Sometimes I think organizations against gaming is made up of hypocrites."

"Let's give them the benefit of the doubt and say they are," Kelly said.

"Now I have a problem. I'm wonderin' if you happen to know a carpenter who could make me a dozen gambling booths. You know, just big enough for one of my lads to occupy. I know they're quite valuable. I'm willing to pay $100 apiece for the master carpenter who could do this difficult job."

"I'm very strong with the hammer," Kane said.

Kelly got up, shook hands with Kane, and walked out. The police chief went down into the basement where they had twenty of the things impounded. He told a patrolman to dust them off a bit. When the grand jury tried to get at him a couple of years later and requoted the conversation to him he said he didn't know what they were talking about.

Kelly, to get the franchise at Sheepshead Bay, gave the Coney Island Jockey Club $5100 a day at the start. He was anything but tough with a dollar. He gave his bet-takers—

sheetwriters, in bookmaking terms—$10 a day, plus carfare and lunch money. He ran a big operation. He averaged $50,000 a day worth of business and at the end of a 20-day meeting at the place he found that, with extra payments and the like, he had given the Jockey Club $136,200, paid everybody who hit him, and still came away with a ton of money for himself.

Sheepshead had the best horses, horsemen, and jockeys in the nation on its grounds. On opening day, for example, three of the nation's top riders were in the jocks' room getting ready for a day's work. One was Edward (Snapper) Garrison, who began what is now known as the Garrison finish. In his day, the Snapper left trainers and owners in a heap while he would stay far off the pace, then close in a rush. The whip in his left hand would slam the horse, his handlebar mustache would flap in the breeze and he would have his cap turned backward. He'd scream at the riders in front of him as he started the Garrison finish. It was fine to watch, but murder on the ticker and one of his owners, a man named Corrigan, wound up in a hospital in Chicago after his jockey just did get up with a mount. Also in the room was Isaac Murphy, a Negro kid who had the arms of a middleweight fighter. Murphy won three Kentucky Derbies before he quit. He won on 44 per cent of his mounts, a staggering figure that nobody has come close to since. And there was Jimmy McLaughlin, a tough Irish kid with a touch on horseback reserved only for a few. McLaughlin went on to win six of the seven Belmont Stakes in which he rode.

New York at this time was a city of a million and a quarter people and everything took a step back to make way for the opening of Sheepshead. The sports world at this time was bare outside of racing. The heavyweight champion of the world, for example, was Paddy Ryan, who came from Tipperary and fought bare knuckles. He won his title by taking out Joe Goss in an hour-and-twenty-four-minute fight at Colliers Station, West Virginia, on June 21, 1880. But nobody knew much about organized boxing in those days and Ryan's victory caused only passing comment in the papers. At that, it wasn't until some days after the fight had been held. The man who was to make boxing popular, John L. Sullivan, was just a thick-chested, fresh guy who could punch good and hung around Boston.

So the newspapers shot the works on what they called the "glorious opening" at Sheepshead. The stories were loaded with words and said nothing for paragraphs at a time. Which isn't a thing that newspapers have gotten over, but in those days there was a good reason for it. Many of the reporters were working on space rates, so when they went on a story they took their best shots. Adjectives, for example, could put bread on your table if you strung enough of them together. The city had a ton of papers, with the *Morning* and *Evening World*, the *Tribune, Press, Mail, Globe, Sun, Morning Telegraph, Times* and *Sun*. Of the people who worked on them, and were knocking out words about Sheepshead Bay the day it opened, everybody was an amateur next to Esdail (Doc) Cohen.

Cohen became an important man in New York newspapers the afternoon Joseph Pulitzer walked into the city room at the *World*, took a look around at a staff which seemed to be industrious, go-by-the-book, and announced he didn't like them at all. "We don't have enough people who drink around here," he said. "Get me a drinker for this paper."

The Doc was made. He had started out in life as a physician in Philadelphia but gave up his practice when he found too many women were having babies during the hours he usually reserved for drinking. He had a flair for writing, so he took down his shingle and came to New York, landed a job as reporter on the *Sun*. His literary specialty, lies, soon earned him something of a name. But he was even more famous for his drinking. When Pulitzer called for a drinker, the *World* editors rated him a 4–5 shot to fill the job. When they finally found him and brought him to Pulitzer there was no question about it. He had been in a place called the Umbrella. By the time he got to Pulitzer's office the whiskey was making him walk stiff and he didn't care about anything but getting the hell out of the office and back to the bar.

"I like drinking," the Doc said. "I drink all the time. You can be sure of one thing. I'm not going to stop." Pulitzer said he was hired and the Doc cut out for a bar. He had just been given a license to drink.

Sheepshead had been running for five successful years before Jimmy Fitz was old enough to get somebody to hire him. And when he did check into the stable area he was a long way from the color and excitement because he was just a kid of eleven working around horses and there was too much to be done in the kitchen and too much harness to be shined and too many hots to be walked to leave room for anything else. He was in the kitchen with the Brannan Brothers for a time and, when that stable headed west, Jimmy Fitz had to hustle around and come up with another spot. This time it was with the powerful stable owned by Phil and Mike Dwyer, two powerfully connected brothers who were as much a part of New York City politics as a ballot box. He weighed a little over eighty pounds when Hardy Campbell, the Dwyers' trainer, took him on as an exercise boy. By now, Jimmy Fitz could ride well enough to fill the job. Like everything else in his life, riding was a thing he had to pick up by himself. Nobody taught him anything in particular, but just by being around stables you learned how to ride, if you were light enough.

The backstretch of a race track at this time was something which, again, is unbelievable today, but was accepted as matter of course by anybody in racing at the time. The stable area was filled with a mixture of small kids who had never received much schooling, and tough older people, along the lines of a fellow named Dynamite, who would pretend he was spitting in some kid's pudding so he could disgust the kid and could have the pudding when the kid walked

94

away. Nearly everybody working at horses put in 83 or 84 hours a week. Apprentice riders were under contract to the trainer, who was supposed to be in charge of not only their working but also he was responsible for their private lives. An apprentice received two meals a day, clothing, a place to sleep, and $10 a month. The trainer saw to it that they were up in the morning and in bed at night. And if they didn't move quickly enough during the day it was nothing for the trainer to give them a swat with anything handy.

It is, of course, all different today. But nobody who came through the old era, particularly Mr. Fitz, thinks there ever was anything the matter with things as they were. It was part of life as it was in those times, and nobody ever claimed the living was easy in 1890 and thereabouts.

The case of a trainer called Bill Daly is an example. Daly was called "Father" because he hit kids. Now this is, as a rule, highly commendable, except the kids Daly hit were not his own. Father Bill kept a pair of rubber martingales—part of the rigging you put on a horse—within reach and whenever anybody in the stable area didn't do as he was supposed to, Daly would take a swipe at him with the martingales.

In 1890, Jimmy Fitz, the kid, didn't see anything wrong with this. And today, Mr. Fitz, in his eighties, still doesn't see where there was any harm done.

"A trainer was in charge of the apprentices," he says, "and these kids were around without any home discipline. They would've gotten a whack or two at home, so what's wrong with them getting it at the track? You say what you want about it, I say there was nothing wrong. And I also say none of these kids got into trouble, the way they do today. There was none of this delinquency. Besides, how are you going to argue with what Daly did? He was as good a trainer as you'll ever want to see."

Daly demanded his jockeys go to the lead immediately and would swing the martingales at anybody from the lowest apprentice to Snapper Garrison if they didn't. The race term,

"On the Bill Daly," which means take the lead right off, comes from this.

He was a tough Irishman who had a peg leg that came in handy at times. There was, for example, one afternoon when he was treating a sore-ankled horse by tubbing him out, as they say, which means you stick the horse's leg into a tub of steaming water. One afternoon while he was doing this, a man from the local chapter of the ASPCA was touring the Gravesend stable area. The ASPCA man was horrified when he saw Daly jamming the horse's leg into the scalding water.

"You're being cruel to that horse," the man said. "I'm going to summon the police."

"It doesn't hurt him a bit," Daly said. "Here I'll show you. I can put my foot in."

"Don't! You'll burn yourself alive," the man yelled.

Daly looked straight at him, stuck the wooden leg into the tub and stood there.

"I told you it didn't hurt none," he told the guy.

Jimmy Fitz had no contract with the Dwyer Brothers. Nobody knew anything about him and they didn't bother to find out if he was worth putting under the apprentice rule. But he still had to work as hard as any kid on the grounds.

The first morning he overslept, the foreman, Theodore Strauss, stomped down the shedrow, counted heads, and saw he was missing.

"Get him up," he yelled.

His assistant knew what that meant. He grabbed a bucket of cold water and climbed up the ladder to the loft and threw it on Jimmy.

"Don't even bother to dry yourself," the guy yelled at Jimmy. "Just get down there and get workin'. Now."

It was 4:30 in the morning and the horses had to be fed. It didn't bother Jimmy Fitz at all. He got up and worked and made sure he woke on time after that.

The Dwyer Brothers put the Fitzsimmons kid to work with their set of yearlings. As an exercise boy, he had to do everything but marry the horses. He rode them mornings, then hot-walked them, fed them, mucked out stalls, helped wash them down, shined the tack and, as a daily rule, did everything but outrun them. This was fine with him until an animal called Aposta, Jr., colt came along. They called a yearling after the mare who produced him in those years. Then they tacked a "Junior" on the end of the name. When the yearling turned into a two-year-old he was, of course, given an official name, except when he began to run in front of people who bet him they usually came up with their own pet names for him. At any rate, the Aposta, Jr., colt came off the farm mean. He wanted nothing more out of life than the chance to bite a hole in somebody's hand or throw an exercise boy as high as possible. He had been in the Dwyers' Stable for two weeks and one morning, while up on another colt, Jimmy Fitz passed Aposta, Jr., just as the colt sent his boy sailing. Jimmy made a mental note to stay clear of this one.

But a few nights later, as he was about to walk into the stable kitchen and grab something, Jimmy heard Rogers, the trainer, talking over coffee with Theodore Strauss, his foreman, about the work lineup for the next morning.

"Who are you going to try on the Aposta, Jr., colt tomorrow?" Rogers asked.

"Jimmy Fitz," Strauss said.

Jimmy Fitz stood like a statue a few steps from the door.

"Little green for that, isn't he?" Rogers asked.

"He's here same as the rest of them," Strauss said. "Let him take his turn."

"I guess you're right," Rogers said.

Not on your life, Jimmy Fitz said to himself. Then he padded away from the door, climbed up to his loft and spent the rest of the night figuring out what ailment he was going to have and what its symptoms were.

The next morning, when one of Strauss' assistants came down the shedrow and yelled up to Jimmy Fitz, the exercise boy announced he was stricken with a stomach ache that was

97

almost certainly an appendicitis attack. He would yell down later if he needed a lift to the hospital for the operation. For now, he'd just stay put.

"It hurts somethin' awful," he said. "I'm good and sick."

"All right," the guy said and he went out and told Rogers that Jimmy Fitz couldn't make the shape.

A few minutes later, however, Lewis, the cook, came down and called up.

"We almost through breakfastin'," he told Jimmy. "You want eats, you better get 'em now."

"I might be able to eat," the kid called down.

"What you want?"

"What you got?"

"Pork chops, fried potatoes and eggs. Some fried onions, too."

"I'll take a little of everything."

Lewis went back to the kitchen and had a tray crammed with food when Rogers looked up from his coffee.

"Who's that for?" he asked.

"Jimmy Fitz."

About five minutes later, Jimmy Fitz, chomping quickly on a piece of bread he was able to grab, was putting one foot into the stirrup on the Aposta, Jr., colt. The colt started to skitter a little and the foreman held tight. Then Jimmy Fitz was on and heading for the track and his mount, who had a mean head on him, did his best to get rid of another exercise boy. The boy lasted through the workout in this case. But he learned that food and lying do not mix at times.

But in general, he found the life wonderful. He was a simple kid who was just starting to read and write a little by picking up a word here and there and writing it down on a piece of paper if he got the chance. He had no grand thoughts of doing anything but a full day's work. The life of a jockey, or of a horse trainer who could go into Allois Soeller's or Billy Schesseler's, the good saloons around the Bay, and be a big man, was a bit more than he could imagine. But he had something going for him. He calls it the horse bug. It means walking around a stable area and seeing one of these huge, graceful animals leaning over to pick at grass with the sun glaring on a strong, beautiful neck that makes a swan seem insignificant. Or listening to the chopping sound of one of them chewing on hay. Or being around them out on the track when their nostrils flare and their legs start reaching out and they move with a smoothness and speed that can be murder on you if you see enough of it. Living and working in Sheepshead Bay meant nothing to him. Only summers of potato picking and winters of long, hard odd jobs and being around the same talk and the same problems and the same dreary life of everybody else who was poor and lived there. The horses made things different. No horse ever could be much in the way of company and when you keep talking about Mr. Fitz loving horses you are getting syrupy. But all through his life every time a horse standing in a stable shifted his feet and made that little *clop-clop* sound it meant something to Jimmy Fitz. It was a sound that got him through life.

This was the start of the long years for Mr. Fitz. He was a little, strong-bodied kid who would travel one of the hardest roads anybody in sports ever took before finally reaching the top. It would leave him with a deformed body and memories of hard work. But it would give him something, too. He is a man who has been part of some of the great stories in sports history, but the hard years in racing taught him that you do not become arrogant or important just because you won yesterday. Tomorrow could start the big slide. The people who learn this lesson are few. But Mr. Fitz understands it and it is something you find running throughout his huge family.

One day last spring, Toney Betts, the New York racing writer, was in the elevator going to the press box at Bowie race track in Baltimore. Jack Fitzsimmons, one of Mr. Fitz's grandsons, was running it.

"I go to law school in the morning," the boy said. "I work here afternoons and then in a law office downtown at night.

99

My wife is expecting a baby so I have to keep hustling. Study? Do that weekends and when I get up in the morning."

"Your grandfather," Betts said, "you don't want to use him."

"My grandfather is one thing," Jack said. "I'm another. I have to make it by myself. I can't go around twenty years from now saying 'my grandfather was Sunny Jim Fitzsimmons.' So I might as well not do it now."

That is Mr. Fitz's creed. And he learned it the hard way.

6.   Rough Tracks

In sports, sometimes it can all happen fast. One minute you have nothing. The next, everything. For a kid named Earl Sande from American Falls, Idaho, it took one minute and 15 seconds to get there. He got on Miss Flame, the first race horse he ever worked in his life, one morning in 1917 at the Fair Grounds track in New Orleans, broke her from the six furlong pole and then, hunched over, his long legs gripping the sides of the horse, he became part of Miss Flame's motion and he worked her in exactly what he was ordered to do—one minute and 15 seconds and not a step faster, kid—and as Sande pulled up Miss Flame, Tom Jordan, the old trainer, clicked his stop watch and turned to the stable foreman next to him and said, "We are going to ride this kid. We're going to do it as soon as we can. He's got a touch." By 1918, Sande had ridden 158 winners and he was around buying real estate.

It happens this way a lot and the stories make professional sports in this country fascinating. But these are stories of the few. For the rest, you nearly always have to tell of long years and hard work, which is the way it went for Jimmy Fitzsimmons of Sheepshead Bay. In the 1880s, a kid working around a race track, as he was, found that there was no such thing as a break, no chance to take it all in one shot. If it ever was going to come, it would come slow.

The Dwyer Brothers Stable was a powerful outfit. Working for them, Jimmy Fitz was around good horses for the first time in his life. From 1886–89, the golden chestnut Hanover was in the barn. He won 17 straight races, earning what was then tremendous money—$109,032.50. By 1886 he had won 14 stakes races before a horse named Laggard, in 17 pounds lighter, beat him at Monmouth Park. Tremont was another big horse in the barn. But Jimmy Fitz was only allowed to look at them—and then only when he wasn't mucking out a stall. The best horse he can remember being on was a mare called Arranger. He worked this one in the mornings. Otherwise, he was a small boy trying to make it in a business and in an era that was tough on men and horses alike.

Anybody working with horses had to be able to do one thing—walk. A trainer named Jack Goldsboro walked a horse from Sheepshead to Morris Park, which is up in the Bronx section of New York, a healthy 25 miles away. Exercise boys and grooms walked their horses from Sheepshead to the Brighton or Gravesend tracks if races were being run there, waited for the race, then walked the horse back. It was a five-mile trip and it could be done two or three times a day and nobody could say a word about it if they got stuck with extra trips.

The horses were not pampered, either. One afternoon in 1889 trainer Billy Lakeland ran a horse called Exile in the first race at Brighton Beach. Jockey Fitzpatrick up, and got nowhere with the proposition. He didn't like it a bit, so he washed the horse down, threw a blanket over his back and walked him over to Sheepshead where he put up Jockey Hamilton and sent the horse out for the sixth race. Exile picked up horses on the last turn, won by a half-length and for his extra effort got a pat on the rump from Lakeland. Away from the track, things were done on the same order. Tim Cochrane, a friend of Jimmy Fitz's, walked up to a place near Prospect Park, eight miles away, bought a stove, had them strap it to his back, then started back. He carried the stove every step of the way. Everybody in the Bay talked about this.

A lot of times, trainers would have their horses worked on the hard sand at low tide along the Manhattan Beach ocean front. The horsemen believed salt water and its natural whirlpool motion was excellent for sore-legged horses, so they would treat an ailing horse by letting him swim in the surf with an exercise boy aboard. Which contributed to a strong aversion to swimming Jimmy Fitz was to carry through life.

Early one morning he was aboard a stable pony taking a swim with the horse through the stretch of ocean between an old iron pier and a beach house that served as a guidemark. Now the Atlantic Ocean, where it touches Coney Island and Brighton Beach, is lake-calm because of the land formation hemming it in. New York would never be a major city if it were not, for one day of rough surf at Coney Island would cut the population in half, New Yorkers swimming as they do. But on this morning, the Atlantic was rolling in with a good thud in every wave. One of them broke hard into the horse's stomach as he tried to climb over it. Jimmy Fitz and the horse went tumbling underneath the water. When they came up, the horse figured it was every man for himself. He pawed at the water to right himself, then he took off for shore. Jimmy Fitz tried one stroke and came to the conclusion he was not a channel swimmer. As the horse's tail swished through the water past him, he reached out and grabbed it and hung on until the horse got him to shore.

There was one afternoon, in the summer, when Jimmy Fitz was at Monmouth Park with horses and he became ill. When his face became flushed with fever, a doctor was called. The doctor took one look and diagnosed it as "chills and fever." This was a synonym for malaria. He pumped the kid full of quinine and then, several weeks later, came around again, listened to his heart, and shook his head.

"You can go home, son," he said. "When you do, you're

going to have to live a different life. Your heart is not strong enough to stand much excitement. You work, don't you. Well, get a nice, quiet job and keep one like that for the rest of your life. Stay as far away from excitement as you can."

Jimmy Fitz said he sure would. Then he took a box of quinine tablets from the doctor, got up and put on his clothes and went home to Sheepshead Bay.

And, on the afternoon of August 17, 1889, which was a year or so after the doctor's warning, Jimmy Fitz was as far away from excitement as possible. He was walking a four-year-old horse named Newburgh into the paddock at Brighton Beach. The paddock was as safe a place as any, he figured.

But things worked differently on this day. Newburgh was to run in the third race with the lightweight assignment of 84 pounds. Hardy Campbell, the trainer, had been looking for somebody to put on the horse all day. Then he looked at Jimmy Fitz, thought about his small body for a moment, then called over to the boy.

"Can you ride this horse?"

"Sure," the kid said, thinking the trainer meant sometime in the future.

"Well, go in and get on some silks and get back out here in a hurry. You're late now."

Jimmy Fitz was stunned, but ran to the jocks' room, then came out dressed in Dwyer Brothers silks, oversized pants and boots, got on the horse and went to the post. In these days, the start of a race was a simple thing. The horses would line up, with no gate or barrier to hold them, then the starter would say "Come on" and the race would go off. This system was bad enough to start the Civil War. In the American Derby at Arlington Park, for instance, the horses were at the post for 90 minutes until they could be straightened out and sent off with no false starts. There was no trouble with Jimmy Fitz's first start. There was plenty when the race began, however. Newburgh simply wouldn't run fast and the jockey was in the midst of a first-mount fog that hits all riders. They finished way back.

This did not make him a favorite around the stable area. Strauss, the foreman, started to pile extra work on him. One day, he had Jimmy Fitz exercise extra horses. When he came back, Strauss still wanted him to shine the same amount of tack everybody else did. Jimmy Fitz said he didn't think that was fair. He was being overworked. Strauss, an understanding man, called him lazy. In a few days Jimmy Fitz's Irish was well up. He packed his clothes and started to walk off.

"Where you going?" an old groom asked him.

"I don't know, but I'm through with this business around here," he said.

"You ought to try the Jersey tracks," the groom said. "I got a friend over there, Pratt. He used to work round here. You go see him. He'll take you on. He needs exercise boys, I know that."

The day he left for New Jersey—a trip in those days—Jimmy Fitz told George Tappen he'd try and dig up a spare job for him.

"The minute I do, I'll write you a letter," he promised.

Tappen wanted to know two things: Who was going to read the letter and who was going to write it.

Gloucester, which is where Jimmy Fitz went, was a small town backing onto the Delaware River. A ferry ran across to Philadelphia. The track and the carnival area adjoining it became known as the Coney Island of Philadelphia, with such added attractions as dice tables, roulette wheels, and places where you could play cards for money in case the Ferris wheel was too crowded. A place behind the Bonaventure Hotel, which was famous for its shad dinners, was the headquarters for Gloucester's gamblers. The town drew a heavy set of Philadelphians, who even at this early date were committing their sins out of town.

The Gloucester track had no particular opening or closing

dates. Normally, a 50-day race meeting is considered plenty for the economy of any one area—except in New York City, where there are enough people to keep anything going. In little Gloucester, however, they ran 580 days at one stretch. Snow, cold, ice, rain; that meant nothing. The only thing that could stop horses from going around at Gloucester was either politics or an absence of money among horse players.

Jimmy Fitz got a job with the trainer, Pratt. When he checked into the ramshackle barn he fixed himself up the same living quarters he had everyplace else—a couple of two-by-fours laid across one corner of the loft, with a straw mattress and a horse blanket over it.

Pratt kept his new boy exercising horses for a couple of months, then decided to try him as a jockey. The minute this was brought up, Jimmy Fitz went to somebody around the barn who knew how to write.

"I hurt my hand the other day, I think," he said. "Would you write a letter for me?"

The fellow said sure. He took out a pencil and piece of wrinkled paper and got ready to write.

"Send it to George Tappen at the Dwyer Brothers Stable in Sheepshead Bay. Tell him he should come over here and valet for me. Tell him I'll find us a place to stay."

The place he found for Tappen and himself was a boarding-house run by Mrs. Alexander Harvey. Jimmy Fitz, Tappen, and a cocky kid named Johnny Tabor, who was riding well at Gloucester, took rooms in the place. Mrs. Harvey had two daughters, Lillian and Jennie.

On September 30, 1890, Jimmy Fitz, a sixteen-year-old kid, was put on a four-year-old horse named Crispin in the fifth race of the day at Gloucester. He broke the horse fast—or, rather, the horse outbroke the jockey, who held on for his life—and was on top by three when they straightened for the run home. Crispin was an easy winner, but the jockey, who was about to win the first race of his life, took a fit and went to the whip. Crispin received a solid beating every step of the way home. The jockey still was slamming away 70 yards past the finish line.

Now the first winner for a jockey is something that sticks in his mind forever. They all can remember the horse, the track, the weather, the people who were there that day, the price the horse paid—the works. But the jockey on this one remembered something else. He came up with the idea that going to the whip on a horse, except when the animal is being lazy, is a waste of time and more harm than good comes of it. As long as the animal tried, Jimmy Fitz left him alone. And today Mr. Fitz demands the same thing of his riders.

After the win on Crispin, for example, he was nursing along a horse named King's Idol in the middle of the pack during one race when Tabor, riding something called John M, pulled alongside. Tabor kept snarling to himself.

"I dropped my whip," he kept saying. "If I had a whip I'd win this thing."

Jimmy Fitz reached across to Tabor and handed out his whip.

"It ain't going to do me any good," he said. "You take it."

Tabor grabbed it and started whacking away. John M took off. Jimmy Fitz was content to hand-ride his mount. He felt the horse was trying and would only resent a belting and sulk because of it. In the stretch, King's Idol started to move. He picked up horses and came on with a rush and Tabor's horse was just able to last and beat him by a nose. With the whip, Jimmy Fitz told the trainer after it, the horse would have stopped dead.

Jennie Harvey never went to any of the races for the first year that she knew Jimmy Fitz. But in January of 1891 they had started to go out a little at nights. On one date, Jimmy and his new girl and Johnny Tabor and Lillian Harvey took the ferry over to Philadelphia to take in a show. With them was Joe Bergen, a tough little Irishman from New York.

Everybody was talking about riding horses during the evening, so Jennie finally decided she'd like to see her friend on the job.

"Do they think it's bad for a girl to go to the track?" she asked.

"I'm there every day," Jimmy Fitz said. "There's nothing wrong with racing, not as long as I'm in it."

She laughed. And the next day Jennie Harvey was sitting in a grandstand seat at Gloucester to see her boy friend ride race horses.

In the third race, a six-and-a-half-furlong affair worth $300 to the winner, Joe Bergen was on Keyser and Jimmy Fitz rode Eddie M. Jennie watched closely. The flag dropped and the field took off. Jennie Harvey was watching the first horse race of her life. Bergen took the lead with Keyser and John Atwood, with a boy named MacAuley in the saddle, was a close second. Then it all happened in one move. Keyser lugged in, hitting the rail hard. The horse bounced off it and went down on top of Bergen. MacAuley never had a chance to steer clear of the mess. John Atwood's lead foot stumbled against Keyser's rump, then his leg gave away and the horse and MacAuley fell on top of Bergen and Keyser. The other horses raced around them and while stablehands rushed out toward the pile-up, Honest Tom, Burrell riding, won the race. Jimmy Fitz was out of the money. Jennie Harvey didn't notice. She had a handkerchief to her mouth. And she was worried.

Back up the track, John Atwood was writhing with a broken leg and the track veterinarian was calling for a guard to shoot him. MacAuley was out cold. Bergen struggled to his feet, swayed a little, but seemed fine. They were more worried about MacAuley. Nobody thought to check Bergen right away. He was bleeding to death inside as he stood there swaying against the rail and watching them try to get MacAuley up. Then the bleeding took the color out of Joe Bergen and he passed out. They took him to a hospital in Camden that night, but it was too late. He died during the night. Jennie Harvey never wanted any part of racing again. By now she had made up her mind that she was going to marry this little jockey. But she was never going to care for a day of his business so long as he rode horses. The day she saw Joe Bergen dying made sure of that.

Lillian and Johnny Tabor were married first and then in June, with twenty dollars in his pocket, Jimmy Fitz was at the altar of St. Gregory's Church in Gloucester and he was saying, yes, he would take this woman.

His honeymoon consisted of getting up to be with horses the next morning and work on them and ride them for short money. And there would be short money for a long time after this, too. But he was young and that would be taken care of some-day, he figured. All that mattered was that he had a sweet, young bride and enough cash to rent a small frame shack on Market Street in Gloucester.

The sweet, young bride, as he was to find out for the rest of his life, was a little bit more woman than she appeared to be. He was taught that after they were married for a week.

Of the few things she brought into the marriage with her, Jennie Fitzsimmons was proudest of a gleaming white linen tablecloth which, on this particular night, she had placed on the kitchen table for dinner. She was at the table, talking with her husband after dinner. Proudly, she ran her hand over the linen tablecloth. Jimmy reached the coffeepot on the stove. It was too hot for his hand, and he hastily put it down on the table. Some coffee spilled on the tablecloth.

"Don't spill things on my tablecloth," Jennie yelled.

"Your tablecloth? What about my hand?" he said. "Never mind your tablecloth."

He poured coffee over the table. He was going to be the boss from the start of this affair, he said to himself.

Jennie started to explode. Then she stopped. There are a lot of ways to get a job done.

"Let's not fight," she said. Then, sweetly: "Would you do me a favor and go into the cellar and bring up some milk?"

Sure, her husband said. He got up and went to the cellar.

(Continued from page 562.)

GLOUCESTER CITY (N. J.)

6th Day—Saturday, Sept. 13th.
Weather bad; track heavy.

Purse $250. All ages. Selling. 1 mile.
OGILVIE & DALTON'S Crispin,
    4; 120 lbs.:....*Fitzsimmons* 1
Tappahannock, 3, 105 lbs..........*Ray* 2
Panama, a, 110 lbs............*Thorpe* 3
  Carbine. 3, 125 lbs.; Tenafly, 6, 110 lbs.;
Ten Strike. a, 115 lbs.; Wayward, a,
115 lbs.; Reform—Algebra, g., 3, 110
lbs.; Littlefellow II., a, 105 lbs.; Little
Moore, 4, 105 lbs. and Black Pilot, a,
105 lbs., also ran. Won by 3 lengths;
4 bet. 2d and 3d.
     Time, 1:51½.

Purse $250. All ages. Selling. ⅞ mile.
E. J. DOWNING'S Genevieve,

Sea Bird, 115 lbs.........
Onondaga—Planette, f., 1

  Truth, 112 lbs.; Colderi
and Castania, 115 lbs., a
by 1½ lengths; 2 bet. 2d ε
     Time, 1:08¾

Purse $250. All ages. 1
G. WALBAUM'S Folsom, 3

Eatontown, 4, 112 lbs....
Glendale, 5, 123 lbs......
  Ofalace, 6, 110 lbs.; I
lbs.; Juggler, 5, 122 lbs.;
5, 122 lbs.; Judge Nelso
and Gounod, 5, 122 lbs., al
by 3 lengths; 5 bet. 2d an

He was halfway down the stairs when he heard the door slam behind him and the lock click.

"Now you can stay there," his wife yelled.

She kept him there for the night. To spite her, Jimmy Fitz opened the big can of milk they kept in the cellar and proceeded to drink most of it during the night. He accomplished much by doing this. He had loaded himself up so much that he knew, by morning, that he was going to be overweight for the day's races. So at 5:30 in the morning, with his wife first unlocking the door, then looking the other way so she wouldn't have to bother talking to him, Jimmy Fitz came out of the cellar and had to get out and hit the road to work up a sweat and lose the weight he had piled on during the night.

"Women!" he said to somebody in the stable area later in the day.

"You're starting to grow up," the guy told him.

As it has been all through his life, there were two sides to the racing business in these days. To Jimmy Fitz, the tracks were tough places to make a living. New Jersey had two of them operating, Gloucester, and up at the other end of the state, Guttenburg, which was on the Palisades, across the Hudson from New York City. As far as he was concerned, they were conducting the best racing they could. It was all he ever wanted out of life, a chance to be around races, and nothing else mattered to him. But Guttenburg and Gloucester mattered greatly to law-enforcement people after a time.

The Gloucester track was three-quarters of a mile around of well-kept running surface. The grandstand was a wooden, single-level structure about 150 feet long. It was covered with a roof. On a good day, a crowd of 1500 would pack the stand and spill out onto the lawn in front of it. The races attracted small fields of six and seven horses and their names were not the flaring, colorful ones of horses on the big time. Owners did not have much time to sit down and think out the name for a horse at tracks like Gloucester so Willie B and Eddie M were far more common than anything along the lines of Equipoise. The purses were small. A race worth $300, of which the winner received $250, was big. Most of them were worth half of that. But it was a place, and so were all the small tracks like it, where you could learn how to take care of horses that run in races. Sam Hildreth and William P. Burch, who could teach horses how to run as well as any men who ever lived, were at Gloucester in this era. And for Jimmy Fitz, it was the place that made him. It would take years before what he was learning was going to show in newspaper headlines and bankbook figures. But he picked up things on these tracks and when he finally brought them to the big-time he was murder.

As long as the weather held up—and it took an outright blizzard to close down the tracks—racing was held every day of the week except Sunday. Holidays were terrific. On Christmas Day, for example, a track owner would throw himself out of bed and rub his hands at the thought of all those people receiving money as presents. It would mean a better handle when the horses broke from the post later in the day. On Christmas Eve of 1890, for example, Jimmy Fitz spent the night in the barn at Guttenburg, got up in the morning and exercised the horses, then rode Once Again in the fourth race, a six-and-a-half-furlong affair worth $400. Once Again finished fourth. It was Christmas only for the stable which sent out Kempland, which took down the $350 first money. For Jimmy Fitz it was just another fourth-place ride.

The biggest job for a jockey was to get paid. On paper, you were to get $10 for each mount, but there were innumerable reasons why you wouldn't get it. To get paid, the jock had to go and collect personally, which wasn't always so simple. A lot of times, a guy with one horse would drop into a track like Gloucester, run him in a race and after it turn his pockets inside out to prove to the kid he didn't have enough money for dinner, let alone paying bills. It was toughest in the winter if you didn't get paid. Because all you would have is a rough bed in a freezing stable and if you looked down the shedrow you could see the steam from the horses as they snorted in the cold air. The first job in the morning was to put your foot onto a frozen bucket of water and start smashing at the ice to break it up so there would be water for coffee and, when it warmed up a little, for the horse.

"It wasn't so much rough riding or anything wrong with the races," he tells you today. "We didn't have any film patrol on us, of course, but about the only difference I can talk about is that once we had a horse stuck in a pocket along the rail we kept him there as good as we could. The jock would holler he needed room or something like that, but we didn't pay him much attention. Once you were in a pocket, you stayed. The tracks mostly were in good condition. They had ground crews out in the cold weather and kept them up. The only trouble was the money. There just wasn't none of it around and you had to go without it most of the time. You'd ride a horse and the fella couldn't pay. Well, what could you do? He'd pay you if you won some money for him on the race. That was the only way you could do it. So you took a chance. Once I got 25 cents as pay for ridin' a horse. I was lucky to get that. I guess if you figure out all the money owed me from all them years it would be about $7000. I sure could have used it then. We had an awful stretch of doin' without. But that doesn't mean I didn't like it. I was around with the horses and that's all I cared about."

But to an awful lot of people, this small-time racing he was around was not a good thing. Through nearly all of its history, and particularly in this era of the 1890s and early 1900s, racing has had to make caution its trademark. Professional world-savers, from the hustler with a store-front church to the influential legislator, always have attempted to use racing as a good example of evil. This is because racing is conducted in public and our custom in this country is to sin in private. In December of 1891, the top turf men of the day formed the Jockey Club, whose main job was to keep racing from spreading out and making too much of a target for do-gooders. The Jockey Club was against all small tracks of the Gloucester-Guttenburg variety. The thinking was that there is only so much money which the public can afford to bet and if there are too many tracks around for them to bet it at, trouble from the outside would be inevitable. The Jockey Club passed a rule that anybody riding, training or owning horses at such as Gloucester or Guttenburg would be banned from appearing at any major track under the club's jurisdiction. Jimmy Fitz had no time to figure out what all this meant. He was making his living at these small tracks and he had horses like Capt. Hammer or Calcium to ride and he stayed at it when the ruling was made. And he stayed for the next eight years, too. The Jockey Club called it Outlaw Racing. To Jimmy Fitz, it was a way to make a living. An honest living, too.

"I'll take an oath," he was saying one night, "that I was only asked twice in my life to do something wrong with a horse. There was one day at Gloucester they had a fella ready to ride this horse called Lancaster and the stewards took him off. They thought something was going on or something and they ordered me to ride him. They knew I gave a hundred per cent all the time. The owner was stuck with me, so before the race he came up and said, 'Listen, we got $800 bet against this horse. There's no way out. If you get beat on this horse I'll give you half the $800.' Well, I told him no. I don't do things like that. I felt bad about it. Was none of my business to ride the horse. The stewards made me. Well, I went out and did all I could and I won the race. It must of hurt them fellas bad. But I couldn't do anything.

"The other time, an owner had a horse I was going to ride and he came to me and said if I won with the horse the bidding would go too high. He had the horse in a selling race—like a claiming race is today—and you had to give five dollars more than the highest bid if you wanted to get him back. Well, he thought the price would get too stiff and he must of wanted the horse. 'Let's get beat this time,' he said. 'I don't do that,' I told him. He was a pretty good fella, you know. He didn't say anything except 'OK.' I forget the name of the horse, but I know how the race went, all right. I win by a head. Incidentally I rode for that owner for many years afterward.

"Now, I been around seventy-six years and these are the only times anybody ever asked me to try something. And for seventy-six years all I been hearing is stories, stories, stories about this and that. It's all nonsense. They make 90 per cent of them up on a rumor. Anyplace I ever was at, they had the best racing they could have and that was about all there was to it."

In several instances, conscientious citizens took it upon themselves to go to work on the race tracks. But it was not an easy thing to do. For wherever there is money, with politicians in the vicinity, many things can be done.

Which was what the Reverend John A. Scudder found one bright February morning in 1891 when he walked into the room used by the Hudson County Special Grand Jury for Gambling in Jersey City. He sat down and awaited his turn to testify. The Reverend Scudder was a man of the Lord and in doing this work he was of the opinion that an anti-gambling law was something that ran coupled with the seventh commandment. So, a year and a half before, he joined an outfit known as the Committee for Law and Order, an outfit of do-gooders who spent most of their time burning because race tracks were running in New Jersey and people were betting at them, in flagrant violation of old state laws.

The Reverend Scudder did not come to make sermons to the Law and Order boys. He was one of those tall, thin, knobby-boned people who surprise you. One afternoon the week before his grand jury appearance, he put on a sweater, pulled a cap down over his eyes to look as vicious as possible, then, a prayer on his lips, headed for the Guttenburg race track. The Reverend walked into the grounds at Guttenburg, just like a sinner, pulled out a dollar and went over to the nearest bookmaker and put it on the Number 3 horse in the first race. Then he fled the place. That night, at a triumphant meeting of his group, he waved the bookmaker's betting slip in his hand. He had enough evidence, he figured, to turn Guttenburg into a good spot for strawberry festivals.

The grand jury filed in and sat down rather stiffly. For a good reason. They were being delivered to the Reverend Scudder direct from barside at a place called Nungesser's, where chief clerk of the court Dennis McLaughlin had bought all the rye and beer chasers needed to rid the *byes* of any morning shakes that happened to be present. The grand jurors all were stand-up citizens who could be expected to do exactly what the situation called for. Any situation. McLaughlin, who just happened to have a side job as full partner of the Guttenburg track, could vouch for this personally. He had spent a week going over names of people he knew well until he came up with enough of them to form a jury. Public indignation over race-track gambling had been so high that he had been ordered to round up a special jury to look into the situation. It cost the race track like hell to help McLaughlin carry out the order, but by the time he reached the "Haytches" on his rolls he had a jury.

The Reverend Scudder began his testimony by producing the betting slip and then recounting how he had obtained it.

"Did the horse win?" a juror asked him.

"I didn't stay long enough to find out," he said.

"That's not enough evidence to prove anything," another juror said. "You're bringin' us hearsay."

A third juror, who unfortunately went into the records nameless, wouldn't stand for this. "It's gamblin' we're after," he snapped. "It seems to me we have evidence of it right here. The Reverend has on his person a bettin' slip. I think he should be indicted for gamin' within the county limits."

The jury voted on the indictment and it took a split decision to get the Reverend Scudder back to his preaching without first having to raise bail. He never bothered to see how the Number 3 horse did.

But this couldn't go on forever. And trouble was coming down on Gloucester, too. Owner Thompson, who lived in an $85,000 palace along the Delaware, was arrested for running gambling late in 1891. Thompson was distressed that his political connections did not make him immune from the pinch. Oh, he was able to handle the charge easily, showing up in court a full year later to plead non vult and pay a $50 fine. But if these Law and Order committees were strong enough to have him arrested, even on a minor charge, it meant that trouble was on the horizon.

But at times, the law came to the track's aid even in sticky circumstances. At Gloucester one day, a Mrs. John J. Tobin, Jr., umbrella held demurely in one hand, sashayed into the betting ring.

"No women here," one of the bookmakers told her.

"I'm going to bet a race horse and I'm going to do it myself," she said.

A track official hurried onto the scene, took her by the arm and began to lead her away. He was explaining that there was a rule against ladies in the betting ring when Mrs. Tobin tightened her grip on the umbrella, then clocked him in the eye with it. The police were called and Mrs. Tobin was brought into court. The judge pondered the case, then said that as far as he was concerned she had every right to be in there betting her money. This gave the track a legal way to allow women to bet—something it never would have tried without plenty of backing.

When you look into these tracks, you get an idea of why people yelled so much about them. For while Jimmy Fitz and the horsemen like him were busy trying to make their small living out of what they thought of as a sport, larceny became the major occupation of many connected with running the places.

A man named Gus Waldbaum owned Guttenburg, for example. For partners he took in not only court clerk McLaughlin, but also one Richard Croker, whose mustache and goatee had become nationally famous since he had taken over Tammany Hall in New York. Croker was the man who was supposed to make everybody forget about the bad things his predecessor, Boss Tweed, had done. After a short time, it was obvious all Croker wanted to do was make Tweed look like an amateur. After running Tammany for five years, for example, Croker was able to put up $750,000 to buy race horses and breeding farms, including a half interest in the famed Belle Meade Stud Farm of General W. H. Jackson. Croker gave the general a quarter of a million in cash on that deal.

Newspapers promptly said that tongues were wagging. "How can Mr. Croker, a poor man only five years ago, now afford to invest such huge money so readily?" the *Tribune* asked. But the tongues never seemed to wag in Croker's presence. He was a man who believed firmly in violence.

Croker's attachment with Guttenburg was for a simple reason. At this time, poolrooms were the main source of gambling revenue in the nation. Many of the places had bookmakers for horse bets and leased wires tapped out results from every track in the country. At Guttenburg, Waldbaum received most of his income from some 320 poolrooms around the East which paid Guttenburg for wired results, plus overnight entries so they could properly book action on the next day's card. The poolrooms paid $10 a day for the service. This gave Waldbaum $3200 a day profit before he even opened the gates. Croker saw to it that New York City poolrooms, which made up the bulk of Guttenburg trade, were solidly lined up with the $10 a day. He was most certainly not an inactive partner. And McLaughlin, aside from murdering any complaints in court, was in charge of seeing that customers had transportation from Jersey City to the track. He hired horse wagons, piled hay across the hard boards, suckers on top of the hay and sent them on their way.

The track seemed to be open for chicanery. There were smart men who sat up nights in Jersey City trying to figure out ways to make some fast money with the Guttenburg operation. Others were doing the same thing in New York. One night, two men appeared at Guttenburg after the day's racing. After identifying themselves as Western Union repairmen, they went to work on the Morse code bugs in the track office. Then one of them went out to the telephone pole which carried the wires out of the track, climbed it and spent the next couple of hours splicing and rearranging things.

It was snowing heavily in St. Paul, Minnesota, the next day, which was January 5, 1892. But at a poolroom known as the Tremont Exchange, John Driscoll, the bookmaker's clerk, was handed a note from his Western Union man. The note said Guttenburg was operating as usual, six races and never mind the snow.

Driscoll went over to a big blackboard and began to chalk in the odds on the day's card at Guttenburg. A horse named Congress in the first race was to go off at 15–1, the Guttenburg overnight entries said.

Then Driscoll started to accept bets. A couple of strangers came into the steamy poolroom, kicked the snow off their boots, then came across the wet floor and put money down in front of Driscoll.

"Congress in the first at Guttenburg," one of them said. He was betting $100. The man behind him had a $50 bet on the same horse.

Driscoll turned around and wiped out the 15–1 next to Congress' name and made it 12–1. When he turned around again, two more strangers were there to bet him. Before he knew it, he had a rush on Congress and the price had to be dropped with every bet. The other Guttenburg starters received little play, although form seemed to dictate a bet on Insight, 8–1, or Flambeau, 5–2.

When the ticker tapped out the result of the first at Guttenburg, it said Congress had won. Driscoll paid off the strangers —who promptly started to bet him on a thing called Mabel, 5–1, in the third race. When the result came in, this horse had won, too. And the strangers were right there to collect and bet it back on Rose G, 18–1, in the fifth.

That night, after closing shop, Driscoll went to get a drink. He stopped into a place called Gleason's, which also had a race wire, and started to knock over double ryes.

"One more day like this," he told the bartender, "and my boss is out shoveling snow. And I'm ringing doorbells to get him the work."

"Bad day?" the bartender said.

"We get ruined by that place in Jersey. Guttenburg. Who the hell out here can pick them at a track like that? I mean, there was guys in today who murdered us on that place."

"What were they playing?"

"Congress," Driscoll said. "That was the one that hurt the most. They are on him at 15–1."

"Congress?" the bartender said. His eyebrows came together. "He was in the first race, wasn't he?"

"Uh huh."

"Hell, he don't win it. Insight win that race. That's what we got on the ticker."

At first Driscoll figured the guy was wrong. He went over and checked the wire. First race, Insight, it said. Driscoll felt

119

weak. Then he looked at the third race. Ma Belle, the winner. The wire notes said Brooklyn took the fifth. Driscoll was a thin fellow who spent his time either in a smoky poolroom or saloon. But he still had plenty of natural strength. You could see that. He did not faint.

In poolrooms around the country, at the Nicolett in Minneapolis and at Malty's in Kansas City, guns were being cleaned and oiled and clerks were being asked to remember faces of those who had bet them on Guttenburg horses that day. The wires, track officials and all else knew by now, had been fiddled with the night before and certain places around the country were hit with phony results from Guttenburg. Bookmakers howled for months. The story reached the papers and more people called for action against the track.

Jimmy Fitz just kept riding horses. He didn't bother with the tales going around. He kept looking for mounts on which he could ride for money.

Another outlaw track of these times opened at Maspeth, Long Island.

Maspeth was built on a picnic grounds owned by a man named Feldman, who had it rigged with lights for the first night horse racing in the country. The big overhead arc lamps were barely enough to lift some of the blackness from the track. More care was given to the lighting of the betting ring, where bookmakers were busy accepting bets on anything that moved anyplace in the country. It was called a Foreign Book in those days and the crowd at Maspeth had as much interest in that as they did in the action on hand. But to keep the crowd informed as to who was leading in the backstretch, Maspeth had a big spotlight rigged up which would hit the leader and stay with him around the track. If the man operating the light happened to be a bit slow, this could raise the devil with the boys riding the horses.

One night, for example, Jimmy Fitz was hustling down the backstretch aboard a horse called Fagan. He was in total darkness. The spotlight man was off the mark at the moment, and Jimmy pushed Fagan onto the lead without any light on him. When the guy in the tower swung the light on Fagan, Jimmy jumped. He saw the shadow of another horse coming up alongside, at a good clip. He gave Fagan a tap with the whip to hustle him up, then he started pumping. He had Fagan under a good drive when he snuck a look out of the corner of the eye to see the horse challenging him. It was his own shadow. To his credit, Jimmy Fitz was keeping a full head in front of it down the stretch. The guy always tried.

In another race, he was aboard a thing called William Penn and the horse stumbled and went down. Jimmy Fitz was thrown off and landed flat on his back. A gray horse named Tommy Lally was striding right at him and one moment there was a flash of the horse's heaving, gray-white stomach, then of his black hind feet skimming past Jimmy Fitz's and then clouds of dirt. The horse had gone over him without touching him. But he still couldn't move. His back had been badly sprained in the fall and they had to carry him back to the stable. The stable area was dark. Grooms carried lanterns as they took horses to and from the paddock and people were too busy to make a big thing of a jockey who fell. Particularly if he had no broken bones. He was out for a couple of days, then got back in action. But his back never was the same after that and through the rest of his life he always remembered William Penn falling and throwing him onto his back. He felt certain, as his back began to bow and his head lowered, that William Penn was the start of his trouble.

While he was at Maspeth, he took the train one fall day to a place called Ozone Park where a new small-time track, called Aqueduct, was opening. Jimmy Fitz didn't have any horses with him that day, but everybody wanted to get a look at the place to see if there was a chance of making money at it. Aqueduct was a wooden place with planks put over the dirt lawn to keep people from sinking into the mud. The track did not look like it was here to stay. He went back to Maspeth.

At this time, around Jersey, the Committee for Law and

Order was making a big move against race tracks—it had staged a successful vigilante raid against Monmouth Park the summer before—and things did not look good. However, the two people for whom Frank Weir was training horses did not seem to mind. They were two quiet guys from the West who had, Jimmy Fitz noticed, better manners than most of the horsemen. "You'd think they was choir boys," he says now. They did not look anything like they did in pictures which federal authorities used to place in post offices around the country. One was Frank James, the other Dick Little, and between these two, and Frank's brother Jesse, they had killed more people than pneumonia.

Finally, time ran out in Jersey. The better people could not be held off forever. The Daughters of the American Revolution were incensed. The WCTU was fighting mad. The ASPCA was howling. And, of course, there were the churches. To any minister or priest not lending his weight against the tracks, it was suggested that Sunday collections were dwindling in areas near the tracks and, given time, the thing could spread. The churches quickly joined the campaign.

By the end of 1893 there were no tracks left in New Jersey.

Which was not good for Jimmy Fitz. A couple of months before, an added starter by the name of John Fitzsimmons had been brought into the world by Jennie Fitzsimmons, who had been in the bedroom of the little house on Market Street at the time. Now, with Gloucester racing gone, the new parent had to find someplace to make a living.

He and Fish Tappen were in the stable area discussing this when one Paul Miles came along. Miles was the owner of a couple of horses. Once in a while he'd win some purse money. The mere fact he and his horses still ate food showed that.

"Well, we can't stay here," Miles said. "I'll tell you, Jimmy. There's racing out at Latonia, in Kentucky. You come out with me and do the riding and we'll split whatever we make. Only thing is, I don't even have the money to ship my horses. Do you, by any chance . . ."

"I'm worried about the week's groceries at home."

"Well, see if you can think of something," Miles said. "If we can get up any money we can go out there."

That night Jennie Fitzsimmons sat and listened to her husband talk about going to Latonia race track if only there was some way to get up the money to ship the horses. The baby was in the bedroom crying. Well, she said to herself, it's a cinch we'll need the crib for another couple of nights. Until it's time to go to Latonia. Well, the crib goes last. But the rest of it? The couch? The chairs? She nodded.

"We'll get to Latonia somehow," she said.

From the day her husband had brought his first married dollar home from the track, Jennie Harvey Fitzsimmons had handled money like it was alive. She nursed it along and cut into a dollar here and a dollar there and before long she had furniture for herself. Nothing special. But it was new furniture and it was her own. This can be very important to a married woman. You'd be surprised just how much it can mean.

When her husband came back from the stables the next afternoon, his wife was making a joke about how much bigger their place seemed without furniture in it. In her hands was a roll of bills. It was enough for shipping to Latonia. This was some woman, you see.

A couple of days later, Jennie Fitzsimmons, her son in her arms, stepped into a coach for the ride to Cincinnati and the Latonia track. Her husband was in the back of the train before it pulled out of the Philadelphia station. He was checking the horses.

When Latonia, across the river in Kentucky from Cincinnati, opened in late May, Domino and Henry of Navarre were putting on one of their great duels in the Withers in New York. Latonia had no such stirring duels of the turf. It did have, however, a rather ancient battle going on. The larceny experts were paired against the suckers and it was every man for himself.

One look around on opening day showed this. To begin with,

123

one of the twenty-seven bookmakers in the betting line, a man who operated under the banner of the Iroquois Club, came on the grounds ready to take friend and foe alike. He was, the papers howled later, "from shaky antecedents." Latonia demanded a $300 payment in advance from all bookmakers operating. This fellow arrived with a check for $150, which was drawn on the East Bank of the Mississippi, or some such place. At any rate, his check was not going to stand up for long once people started mailing it around. He also handed the clerk a sealed envelope which was supposed to contain the other $150. All it really contained was a $5 bill, plus some assorted cuttings from the local gazettes.

Our man lasted seven-eighths of one race. When the favorite, which was going to pay $8 or thereabouts, and which had been played heavily with our man, started to come on at the eight pole and was most certainly going to win, the gentleman from the Iroquois Club did 22.4 for the furlong between his stand and the exit gate. There was the devil to pay over this. He did not, of course, forget to bring all the money with him.

In the next race, James Fitzsimmons was listed as jockey on a horse called Simrock. With Miles' two horses in the stable area, they would go in a day or so, he had been able to get an opening-day mount from a man named Frank Brown, who had shipped Simrock up the Ohio River by boat from Louisville early in the morning. Unfortunately, Brown was considered a stranger at the track, too.

His horse had been made favorite on the opening line. But an hour before post time, while Jimmy Fitz was sitting in the jocks' room, a groom was talking gently to Simrock as the horse lapped up a bucket of water he had in his hands.

"What you doin' that for?" somebody called from down the shedrow.

"To make him run slow," the groom said.

He was following explicit instructions which had been given

him by one of the track officials. The orders were to give the
horse water or get off the grounds.

There are many things which contribute to a horse's slow-
ness, but nothing does the job quite as well as a bucket of
water right before a race. And when the flag dropped to start
the third race and the field took off, Jockey J. Fitzsimmons
found he had under him something which was moving about
as fast as a beer horse.

He finished way up the track. The minute he dismounted,
the judges were waiting for him, too.

"You didn't let the horse run," one of them, Judge Price,
snapped. "We don't want you or any of your connections
around here. Pack up and get out."

Brown then was called before them. "What are we, hicks?"
Price said. "That horse couldn't run because he was broken
down. Get off the grounds."

Judge Price was, at this moment, standing up for a group
of bookmakers who had come up with a formula to make a
small fortune at the track. They had, it was disclosed weeks
later, placed all the jockeys under instructions. Whoever the
books said was to win either won or somebody would be
mangled. It was a wonderful setup and it included no room
for a Fitzsimmons.

At the end of one day at Latonia, then, Jennie Fitzsimmons'
furniture had gone for nothing more than a train ride. Her
husband and Miles had been ruled off the track and now
everybody was stranded in Cincinnati. When Jimmy Fitz went
back to the hotel to tell her about it, she was holding the
baby.

"Oh," she said. Nothing else.

The journey from Cincinnati to the Union Station in Wash-
ington, D.C., which is where the Fitzsimmons family and
Tappen headed to make a fresh start—a half-mile track at
Alexander Island, Virginia, had just opened—took three days.

The night they arrived in Washington, Jimmy Fitz and his
wife, who had John in her arms, took a room in a hotel on

125

Pennsylvania Avenue. The place was crawling with bedbugs and they had to spend the night brushing them off the baby. Back at Latonia, the papers were filled with stories about how the bookmaking ring had been broken up at the race track. Jimmy Fitz didn't even know about it and if he had been told he wouldn't have cared. He never was a guy who looked back. Besides, he knew he had an awful lot of days ahead of him which could be tougher.

7. Sweating It Out

The train was the Cincinnati Limited *and the Pullman porter had been told to take extra good care of Mr. Sunny Jim Fitzsimmons, who was in Bedroom A and was a very important man because he was on his way to Churchill Downs to run Bold Ruler, the favorite in the 1957 Kentucky Derby.*

It was right after dinner when the porter came around for the first time and stuck his head into the bedroom.

"Anythin' I can do for you, Mist' Fitzsimmons, you just leave me know," he said.

"Oh, I'm fine."

"We near Philadelphia now."

"Oh, I know that. 'Cept when I was down around here before I didn't have people askin' me what I wanted. I was lucky to be gettin' eats."

"You need financin' in those days, huh?"

"I wasn't worried about money, son. I just wanted to get enough eats."

By the time he arrived in Washington, getting the food was only part of the problem for Jimmy Fitz. The hardest part was making sure he wouldn't eat it.

"Irisher," an old man at Alexander Island told him one day,

"Irishers, they grow late. Looks to me like you just startin' to grow. Now you do one thing. Don't you try and stop it."

But he did. In the mornings, after working horses, he'd pull on extra sweaters and jog around the track. He stayed away from water, but the stable area became a torture for him because you always had a boy drinking water from a spigot or pouring it over a horse and just to look at this made Jimmy Fitz thirsty. At meals, he would sip black coffee and eat sparingly—he would eat lettuce only after Jennie had dried it out in the sun. The weight didn't simply come on suddenly. It was something that had been happening to his body little by little. A half pound here, a few more ounces there. But it was coming to stay. From the time he was eighteen, Jimmy Fitz should have weighed 140 pounds, even if he were working on a construction job. Instead, he was riding horses who were assigned 113 pounds or 115 or 116 or 118 and only sometimes would there be a break and a horse in with 126 or 130 would be available. So he fought weight to make a living. Anybody who ever has had to do it knows it is one of the most terrible battles you can take on.

It is an awful way to live and not many people understand what a jockey who is gaining weight goes through. It is a primeval thing—man against his body. If you walk on any race track in any year and look at what it does to these little men you can see it. The faces tell you. The eyes are hollow and and have black smudges under them. The cheeks sink in and the skin is dry and it looks gray. The meals are always the same. A little black coffee in the morning, a piece of meat, no gravy, some spinach and a little more coffee at night. Some of them don't use their heads and go out at night and load up with food, then duck into the washroom and bring it up by sticking a finger down the throat. They figure they're fooling their stomachs. In the mornings they use steam baths and it dehydrates some of the heavier ones so much they scream to an attendant for a bottle of soda. He punches a thin hole in the top with an ice pick and the kid sucks on the cap, getting a thin stream of the liquid into his throat. If the cap was taken off completely, he'd swallow the whole bottle full of soda in two gulps and it would be too much weight-registering liquid. He'd have to go into the bathroom and bring it up. Sometimes, on a hot day, their bodies begin to sear during a race. Between races, the kids pile naked into a tub full of ice cubes. Only the years they have to live will tell them what it does to their bodies. The way the years told Jimmy Fitz.

The weight was making it impossible for Jimmy Fitz to get mounts. He began to take on any job at the track which would pay him a quarter. He worked horses for trainers, then now and then they'd have a "Cook's Race," which was for heavy jocks, and he would be in these. He and Jennie had taken a couple of rooms in South East Washington at the time and they had a house guest, his brother Pat, and since Pat wasn't doing too well in his ventures around the track, the whole operation was in bad shape.

One afternoon a heavy-set guy named Murphy, who came from Philadelphia and was in the building business, arrived at Alexander Island to bet a race horse or two. Murphy, who had been a regular in the Gloucester days, was standing around the track office when he bumped into Bill Mosley, who was training one or two horses.

"You got a filly named Luray?" Murphy asked.

"She's not a bad one," Mosley said.

"I know," Murphy said. "And she fits that race tomorrow real good. This one here on the sheet, the fourth. I'd like to make a bet if I knew what kind of a ride I was going to get. I'll bet a hundred-dollar bill for you and the jock if I can get the right ride."

"Who do you want up?" Mosley said.

"I'd like to go with that Jimmy Fitzsimmons. Haven't seen him since Gloucester closed. But I know he gives you the right count. If you can get him, I make the bet."

"I'll get him," Mosley said.

Jimmy Fitz was in the stable area and he was weighing

exactly 118 pounds when Mosley hustled up to him with the proposition.

"We're in at 108," Mosley said. "If you can make 105 or so, we got a chance to win $100 bet. For a square meal I'd run in the race myself."

"I'll be here tomorrow. And I'll give her the best ride I know how," Jimmy Fitz said. Then he got going. He had to get 13 pounds off a body that didn't seem to have an extra ounce on it. And he had only 22 hours to do it.

He walked out of the track, crossed the bridge into Washington and went home to start the lonely business of reducing. To prevent any real hunger from coming on later in the day, he swallowed a cup of tea and piece of toast in his kitchen. Then he went to the cabinet and got out the equipment he needed. He filled a glass full of salt, then added water. He stirred the mixture, then set it out on the table. Later, when he came back, he would knock it down in one swallow. The salt water was a strong laxative. He also took out a pint bottle of rye whiskey and poured a couple of fingers into another glass and put it alongside the salt. The whiskey was important. It would go down right after the salt to kill the gag in his throat the laxative always produced. His brother Pat sat in the kitchen and looked at the whiskey.

He left the two drinks side by side on the kitchen table, then mumbled to Pat and walked uptown to a Turkish bath on Pennsylvania Avenue. He paid his way in, got undressed and then walked into the hottest room in the place. He sat down and pulled himself together for the long wait. At 7 P.M., when they came around and said the place was closing, Jimmy Fitz, his tongue thickening and his throat feeling like paper, came out, toweled himself, and headed home. An attendant was drinking from a fountain as he went down the hall and Jimmy had to look away from him. All he could think of was drinking the salt solution when he got home. He had to close his eyes when he thought of how it tasted.

When he walked into the kitchen at home, he didn't talk to

his wife. He just reached for that salt water and got the thing over with. It went down very bad. He did not like the taste of whiskey, but it was a sure chaser for the salt. He flipped the glass of rye into his mouth. The minute the stuff hit his tongue he started spitting. It was cold tea. When it mixed with the salt taste it was vile.

"Where's Pat?" he demanded.

Pat was not around. He had been earlier.

Jimmy Fitz, disgusted, went to bed. Between tossing and turning under three blankets during the hot night and getting up early, putting on sweaters and a muffler, and working horses, he had a fair chance to make the weight by mid-morning. He had lost eight pounds. To lose the last few, he went out on the road in front of the race track when training finished at 10 o'clock and started walking and running in the hot sun. A few miles down the road, a fellow bare to the waist in the blazing sun was working at a brick kiln. Mr. Fitz stopped there and stood in front of the white-hot fire for an hour. The sweat soaked his heavy winter clothes as he baked himself. Then he started back for the track. He hadn't put a thing down his throat all day. And now he was sagging a little. But he could tell by the weight of his sweat-heavy clothes that he had lost pounds. The scale confirmed it. He did 105 for the race. To Mosley and Mr. Fitz, it was a helluva thing. They were talking about what a job it had been when Murphy, the bettor, came around. Murphy didn't care about the weight or any tales to do with the subject. He had a good word on another horse in the race. His personal figures gave the horse a good shot at it, better than Luray, he said, and he had decided to change his move.

"I'll do business with you fellows another time," Murphy said. "I got a strong word on this AOH and I'm going to put my money where my figures are."

Mosley had to talk like a guy trying to get the rent, which is what he was doing, and Murphy reluctantly decided that he was stuck; he'd stand up and bet the $100 on Luray.

As the race was called, Jockey J. Fitzsimmons stepped up to the scale and carrying his tack (saddle, saddle cloth, weight pad, and whip) stopped the needle at 108 pounds. He hit the weight limit on the nose. Then he stepped off and headed for the paddock.

"That kid dropped 13 pounds since yesterday," somebody whispered as he walked off.

"Crazy," the clerk of scales said.

"You don't know this one," the guy said. "He's broke. And he just won't get out of the business. Has to be on a race track. He's got the bug all right."

When the race started, the dice finally came up seven for Jimmy Fitz. He saved ground all the way around and at the top of the stretch he had a live mare under him and he got on the head end. But Murphy's figures were not too far off. AOH was battling for it all down the stretch and Luray just got home by a nose. The horse had gone off at 8–5. Later, he and Mosley split a little less than $160. They had pulled off an impossible thing and they both felt good about it.

Jennie Fitzsimmons felt good when her husband came home with the money, too. She talked with him over the dinner table and made him eat a meal and the two of them forgot all about Pat's whiskey drinking. Jimmy Fitz's body hurt him all over, but he didn't care. He never mentioned any of the twinges in the upper part of his back. He had dried himself out to the point where the marrow of his bones lost all moisture and the first little bit of arthritis which today bends him over took hold on his backbone. But his legs pained, too, and so did his head and his arms. He never noticed the back pains too much.

Around Washington at this time there was a big ex-butcher named Frank Herold, who was trying to make it with horses any way he could—owning them, training them, or betting them. Whatever road he took was always bumpy. On Thanksgiving Day, for example, he came back from the track and walked into his cheap hotel with a growl in his stomach. He could use a meal. Three other horse guys jammed into his room upstairs were in similar shape. Herold was busy wondering why he was silly enough to pay hotel rent when he could be sleeping in the stable at Alexander Island when the desk clerk called him over and gave him a package sent by a man from Brooklyn.

Herold remembered the name, Gurfein. Mr. Gurfein, some weeks back, had come to Washington from Pitkin Avenue to see such things as the Smithsonian Institution, the U. S. Treasury and other sights. But he had contrived to spend all but a few hours of his time around the paddock at Alexander Island. Herold had touted him on something that, surprisingly, won at a good price. Gurfein went back to Brooklyn and told everybody Washington was a beautiful city. He never forgot his sightseeing trip.

His package, Herold found, contained a cooked turkey. Frank took it upstairs, put it on the bed and in a matter of minutes the bird had bones clean enough to stand in a museum. Herold looked at it for a moment.

"Give me some change," he asked one of them in the room.

Herold wrapped up the bones, went downstairs and bought some postage stamps, then mailed the package back to the guy in Brooklyn.

"We'll see if he can take a hint," Herold said.

Jimmy Fitz and Frank Herold met and spent time with each other at Elkton, Maryland, and from there they decided to go out and hit the Maryland Outlaw Circuit together. This was a group of small tracks around the horse-conscious state. They were called Elkton and Herring Run and Barksdale and Patuxent and the Iron Hill tracks and at any of them there was not much left over after the horses were fed. He and Herold had a loose partnership, which no money was threatening to pry apart because everything seemed to be like it was at Patuxent, Maryland.

A man named Jones had a tomato farm outside the little town. He had heard so many tales about how much money you could make with a race track that he decided to get into the business. He began by scratching out a rough dirt track around one of his tomato patches. The track had a pretty good dip in it halfway down the backstretch. Then he put up a few rows of bare wooden grandstand seats, contacted a couple of bookmakers to handle the action, then sent out announcements of his track opening. Herold and Jimmy Fitz and Tappen came on the grounds, shipping in from Elkton. They thought it would be a little better chance to get some money than they faced at most places.

On opening day, while Tappen and Jimmy Fitz went to the makeshift jocks' room, Herold toured the plant. And he did not like what he saw. There were only about fifty people out for the races. Most of them were local farmers who might bet a dollar or two, but then again, as will farmers, they might not. The two bookmakers on the grounds were shocked. Owner Jones looked worried. Herold figured it was a day where only the alert would survive.

Herold and Jimmy Fitz were in with three horses, Farragut, Dewey, and a mare called Wistful. Wistful, Fitzsimmons up, won a six-and-a-half-furlong race in the second and Herold thought it now was time to be alert. The jockey was just climbing off the horse when Herold was on his way to the track office. He was a little too smart to ask for money. He ran the risk of getting a stall if he wanted cash for the winning race. Instead, he asked offhandedly for an order on Jones' store for fifty dollars' worth of feed for the horses and food for Jimmy Fitz, himself, and the rest of the crew. He got the order, went on the double to the store and presently was back in the stable area with enough to feed everybody. It was one of the big moves that can save a man's life. For the bookmakers gave it up early and went home and everybody else running horses at the track was given a particularly sad story by Jones. Herold and Jimmy Fitz were the first, last, and only people on the track to get anything more.

For a woman, the life was no good at all. You don't make a

big production out of anything when you scrape for a living and Jimmy Fitz and his wife would come into a town, take a rented room, maybe two rooms if they had any money, and when it would come time to ship to another town, Jimmy Fitz would go first with the horses and she would follow by rail. Moving the furniture was no problem because there wasn't any. But she never complained at all. Mostly, she was too busy trying to help. She was a woman with the strength of a brick. She sewed dresses to make money and also made thin, whipcord jockeys' pants by hand, which her husband took to the track and sold.

"I'd hold out on her once in a while, too," he says. "But she never squawked. Figured it was gone to feed a horse or something. Mostly, that was the case, too."

A doctor in Philadelphia, Baird Murray, a confirmed horse player and friend of Fitz's from the Gloucester days, used to give his old suits to Jennie and she'd cut them down and fix them up for her husband. Since a doctor's suit never gets worn too badly, and she was good at sewing, Jimmy Fitz on his worst days was able to dress as if he had it made.

It was, on the whole, nothing more than a bare life for Jennie. By now her mother had died and her father had married a woman everybody in the family called Aunt Amanda. They were living in Frankford, a residential section in northeast Philadelphia, and Jennie went there whenever her husband would be on the road for any extended trip. She was raising a family, too. Her second son was named Jimmy. The third was named George. Both came into the family when she was living in Frankford. Her husband was not present for either birth. Jimmy Fitz was too busy making the three or four dollars that he would put into an envelope and mail home every day or so to take time out. Packing up and heading home for a new baby was out of the question. There wasn't enough carfare.

When he came home he liked to sit in the living room and watch how the kids learned to walk. He was very interested in their stride and which leg they led off with and how they made a turn and things like that. All of which would infuriate his wife.

"These children are not horses," she would say.

This is a habit which has not left Mr. Fitzsimmons so far. When somebody comes up to say hello to him, he'll put a clock on the guy as he walks up and his greeting of times will be, "Morning, Jim. You're walking wide today."

All of his race riding has carried over to almost everything else. From the day they invented the automobile, for example, this has been America's worst back-seat driver. There was one morning a while back when Mr. Fitz was going along crowded Liberty Avenue, outside of Aqueduct, with son Jimmy driving. He began to harp on Jimmy's ability at the wheel.

"Don't get right in behind that other car," he said. "Lay off to the side there. Then you'll be in position. If this car in front stops for some reason, you'll have to stop, too. Get off to the side where there's some running room."

"If he thinks he's on a race track with this machine, that's fine with me," a guy riding with him said. "But tell him if we brush against the rail we're all going to spend the month in traction." He pointed to the "L" pillars the car was skimming past.

This kind of thinking comes from years of doing nothing but being with horses, of course. Which is all he could do, in these tough years. He had no outside life. If they were going to eat, Jennie Fitzsimmons had to stay home and try and raise children and pay a few bills and stall the others without even moral support. Her husband had to be away. It didn't make it easy, but it was the only way it could be done.

In Frankford, when George was two, he disappeared one morning and couldn't be found. His mother searched the neighborhood, then gave that up and called the police. The kid was finally found at the end of the day—sleeping behind the living-room couch. It was one of those things that happen when you have kids and it doesn't seem like much, except she had to go through this fright alone, and all the cuts and accidents that followed it. It is no bargain to raise a family without a husband around. And when Jimmy Fitz was away, his communications consisted of an envelope containing the couple of dollars, plus a note that was written in Sanskrit.

"She had a helluva time trying to figure out most of it," he says. "I wasn't much on the writin' and words for a long time, you know. So when I was away, I'd be away. There was no telephone or anything like that. One time I got a chance with a couple of horses some fellas owned and I went to New Orleans with them, I was training 'em, and I was down there for three months. If anything happened, I couldn't of done much about it."

Wherever he traveled, the cards came up as bad in one place as they did in the next. In New Orleans, for example, he got nothing. The Fair Grounds was a major track and Jimmy Fitz wasn't licensed to be on a place like this—he was outlawed at any major track—so he got another trainer on the grounds, John McKessey, to put his name on the entry blanks for the couple of horses Fitz was handling. Jimmy had one shot at the meeting, when he got a horse named St. Lorenzo ready for a race. He and McKessey got up a couple of dollars and bet the horse, but a jock named McIntyre was on him and didn't do much of anything in the race except lose it. Nobody ate much that night around the horse's barn.

Johnny Tabor was on the grounds when the horse was ready to go the next time, so Jimmy Fitz got him to take the mount. His brother-in-law did a good job. The track was tough going along the rail, but there was a path on the outside and Tabor followed it all the way around to get home on top. But the stewards blew up at the form reversal—one time out of it, the next a winner—and suspended the horse for being "erratic and acrobatic." Jimmy Fitz had no way to argue the issue simply because he didn't know what erratic and acrobatic even meant. So after three months, he had nothing to show. When a smallpox epidemic broke out in the town, he headed for home.

The days, then, all were bad and one seemed like the next because the horses all were a little slow and the money always was short and the food skimpy. And the days kept turning into years. But through all this, one thing about the man kept standing out. He was being taken by larceny, he knew what it was and there could have been chances for him to try it himself. This doesn't mean he could have gotten out of the hole by doing some stealing with horses. But he could have made it a lot easier on himself every step of the way. Yet he never gave it a try. His reason is simple. Back when he was six or seven, or maybe even eight, you see, he had learned what he thought was the difference between right and wrong. Nobody had ever bothered to tell him what was the good way to do things and what was the bad way. He had watched other people and made up his mind how he was going to act. He was not going to steal, for one thing. Nor was he going to complain. Nor were you going to find him putting the finger on anybody else. He had made up his mind he was going to take everything as it came and never look left or right.

"I had to do everything myself," is how he puts it. "Anything I did I was proud of. Well, I had to find out right from wrong by myself. But I did learn it. And when I did you couldn't change me for the world. I was proud I knew something and I wasn't going to go back on it. What I did know I wanted to keep. Lord knows, I didn't learn much."

At Barksdale, Maryland, for example, he was training a horse named Electro. He put a jock named Charley Zeller on him for one race. The track was thick mud along the rail, dry and hard in the middle. Zeller got stuck in the goo and lost. After the race the people who owned the track, two gambling house operators named Mackie and Marks, suspended Jimmy Fitz.

"They said I'd been doping the horse all the time and I didn't give him the hop to win this time," he explains. "The dope was news to me and the horse, but there was no sense complaining any."

Electro happens to be one of his all-time favorite horses. He got the horse with money put up by Dr. Murray. For years, the doc was one of Jimmy Fitz's hole cards. Murray was a tobacco-chewing, horse-playing general practitioner who got to like the way Jimmy Fitz rode horses back in the Gloucester days. The two became friendly after that. Murray always kept loose money in a desk drawer in case a chance came up to invest in a horse, either with a bet or a purchase. He put up the money to buy Electro and Jimmy Fitz first rode the horse on the Maryland circuit, then trained him and ran him and the horse kept putting pork chops on the table for a couple of years.

He and Herold had a ton of uninvited trouble with a horse called Superstition. In their scuffling from one place to the other to make a living, the two wound up out at Latonia with the horse. And the horse had brought along a slight problem. Superstition simply would not run well the first time over a race track. But give him that race over the track and put him back and he was a tough horse. They put Superstition in the first time and got nowhere. A few days later, when entering the horse again, Jimmy Fitz told Herold to ask the stewards to have the horse declared out of the betting.

"He's in real good shape and he's liable to come close and it'll be a bad form reversal. Get him out of the betting and we have nothing to worry about."

The stewards refused, Superstition won like a good thing at telephone number payoff prices and Latonia once more blew a fuse over ex-jockey now trainer James Fitzsimmons.

By 1900, things were even worse. The Maryland circuit had dried up, Fish Tappen had given it up and was working in a livery stable in Philadelphia, Jennie Fitzsimmons was living in Frankford and her husband was living in a small shack outside the grounds of a half-mile fairgrounds place called the Eagle Track, which was at Media, Pennsylvania. He and Herold were trying to make it with three horses around the small fairgrounds tracks at Marcus Hook, Oxford, Pennsylvania, and the like, but if it weren't for a little outside help they might not have lasted.

The help came from (a) an apple orchard bordering on the track, (b) a man who bought up cows from the surrounding area, then sold them once a month and didn't care to be in the milk business so he gave away all milk, and (c) Herold's native ability to talk to another butcher.

The Fitzsimmons-Herold cook tent was set up alongside one run by Johnny Fox, who had a stable of horses, a complement of help and an endless line of stories to give the help. Fox's help were given mostly varied types of stewed fruit for their meals. If it weren't for the orchard they might have gotten a lot less. But over a period of months, Herold had been buying 15 cents worth of ham nubs from a general store outside the track and by dint of continual and affable appearances he soon had it to a point where for 15 cents he could get a nub with enough meat on it to make a meal of ham and cabbage for he, Fitzsimmons, and the one or two rubbers who always were around.

This led, one night, to a minor disturbance in the Fox stable. Monty, who was one of the sensitive members of the operation, particularly where his stomach was concerned, looked up from his cooked fruit one night and, his head going back and forth like a cat, followed Frank Herold's fork from ham and cabbage plate to mouth and back again.

"Mister Johnny," Monty finally said. "What about a little of that ole ham for Monty here? He get hungry jest like them fellows over there do. He'd also like to eat jest like them fellows."

"You want *ham?*" Fox said. "Don't you know any better. You get the scurvy from ham. That's why we're eating fruit here. There's scurvy all over the place and we're eatin' fruit to keep it off of us."

"Scurvy's fine with me," Monty said. "Jest long as I gets it off of that ham they eatin' over there. Mister Johnny, right now my stomach, it begging for a good case of scurvy."

One of the lone bright memories of the whole Eagle encampment came when Dr. Murray, around for a visit, started to argue with one Iz Meyers about the merits of the Fitzsimmons horses as against Meyers' Dutch Lady. A $10 match race was arranged and Jimmy Fitz, aboard Farragut, won it. The ten was a whopping purse for him. Mostly, they were smaller. For one tiny meeting at Marcus Hook, 30 miles away, Jimmy Fitz walked there and rode a horse for a man named Miller. He finished second and Miller received a purse of five dollars. Jockey Fitzsimmons, for pay, took 25 cents.

For the first time in her life, Jennie Fitzsimmons decided to step in. She had given up on the business of running horses. Jennie spoke to Aunt Amanda. This was a forceful person and she went right to work. Aunt Amanda put the arm on her nephew, who had a better-than-average job with the Philadelphia Traction Company. By the time Jimmy Fitz knew anything about it, Aunt Amanda was ready to fit him for a motorman's glove. Aunt Amanda thought it was great. Running a trolley car every day was the kind of a job she could understand. Jennie was all for it, too. Her husband was going to get $15 a week. And he'd go out and work his shift on the trolley, then be home to take care of things like any other husband. She had no use for horse racing from the day she saw Joe Bergen, the jockey, die at Gloucester. She had learned to dislike it more in the last few bleak years. She was all for the trolley car.

To Jimmy Fitz, the Philadelphia Traction Company's shiniest, best-conditioned trolley car, bell well tuned and all, bore a striking resemblance to a cell block. A horse, even a patched-up, sagging old thing trying to navigate around a ramshackle track like Barksdale, had much more to it than any trolley car. Furthermore, old ladies, the kind who like to argue when you forget to tell them at what stop to get off, are not found around horse barns. But if he was going to keep his life with horses, it would have to be under some arrangement where he would be around his wife most of the time. And he would have to at least match the $15 a week the trolley car would produce. Also, any move he was going to make in the direction of horses would have to border on cloak-and-dagger because Aunt Amanda had a strong finger on those trolley cars and she was not about to give up on it.

A fellow named Hughie Hodges, who was a trotting horse man, saved the whole thing. Jimmy Fitz met him one day at about the time Aunt Amanda's nephew was getting the OK to hire a new motorman by the name of James Fitzsimmons. Hodges was working for a Colonel Edward Morrell, a money guy from the Torresdale section of Philadelphia who had a big farm on which he bred and raised a few thoroughbreds. Hodges trained them for him. Morrell needed an exercise boy and jockey for the small set of horses and Hodges figured Jimmy Fitz would fit in fine. All he'd have to do is lose weight —he was up to 1331/2 now—and things might work out. Jimmy Fitz wasn't about to wait. He started walking for Torresdale. It wasn't wasted steps.

The deal with Morrell was fine. He had one of those big, almost feudal kind of estates. His wife had a small schoolhouse built on the property, in which she taught school for the children of those working on the grounds. She came from the Drexel family, not exactly the minor leagues. Under the terms of Jimmy Fitz's deal, he was to work with the horses, losing weight and getting in shape to ride, and live on the grounds with his family. Then in the spring he'd ride Morrell's horses at the big tracks, Sheepshead Bay, Morris Park, and the like. Morrell would see to it that Jimmy Fitz was reinstated as a rider on the big tracks. Financially, the deal came to a little bit better than the $15 a week the trolley car would have paid. So he took it. Aunt Amanda snorted when she got the news, but there was no talking him out of it.

During the winter months, he went on a starvation diet, knocking his weight down to 108. He also began to show he had a special way with horses. A mare called Flexing had a club foot which made her helpless. Morrell's veterinarian had decided to destroy the horse, until Jimmy Fitz went to work on her. He built a special plate for her, then nursed the horse along as the foot began to grow and straighten with the special shoe. Before he was finished she could run in races. Everybody thought it was a miracle.

Morrell had Jimmy Fitz reinstated as a rider with the Jockey Club, so on August 7, 1900, he was back at Brighton Beach again, this time with the filly Agnes D. He won a race with her, his first ever in New York. It is a date which should be important because it marked his return to the big-time. But it really doesn't mean that much because he still had years to go before he was going to make it. Any luck he had was only temporary. As was his riding. He lasted until 1901 when he rode Agnes D in the Tidal Stakes at Sheepshead Bay, finishing last in a race that was won by Water Boy, ridden by George Odom, who went on to become a big success as a trainer. Jimmy Fitz simply couldn't hold off weight any more. So he trained Morrell's small string, which included a jumper named Betsy Ross. This one made up for a lot of bad luck by winning a two-mile steeplechase race at Morris Park under the weirdest of circumstances. When the field broke, it began to look good. Twelve started in the race, but as they hit every jump the number decreased. Two horses would fall at this jump, a couple would go at the next and finally there was only Zenith, a smooth-moving animal which was a good 30 lengths in front, and Betsy Ross. Zenith took the last jump easily, then rolled down the stretch to win. Betsy Ross plodded down after the leader. But when the horse got back to the winner's circle and the jock weighed out, they found that 12 pounds of lead had slipped from his saddle during the race, so he was disqualified. Betsy Ross, J. Fitzsimmons trainer, was the winner.

He stayed with Morrell until 1906. Then he decided to try

143

his scuffling, get-a-dollar-anyplace way of life around Sheeps-head Bay. He moved his family to the Bay, where they stayed with his sister Nora who, after the death of their parents, had taken over the job of running the family. Jimmy Fitz hustled a couple of horses to train and it was Maryland all over again for him, except he was home.

Racing in New York at this time had a splendor and color about it that few things in this country ever have had. They ran six races a day at the big tracks, starting at 2:30 and end-ing at 5:30. The people with money rode down to Sheepshead Bay in classic coach-and-fours, parked their carriages in the infield from where they watched the races. It was gracious liv-ing, studded with some of the flashiest operators ever to take a shot on a horse.

One of them was a fresh-faced kid from Pittsburgh who got a job for three dollars a week in New York, then decided to try the race tracks now and then because he had a notion a man who took jockeys into consideration when he bet a horse might do pretty well. His name was George Smith, but when he died at thirty-eight and left three million dollars, people all over knew him as Pittsburgh Phil. The first time anybody remembers him getting into big action came the morning of a match race between Volante and Dew Drop at Sheepshead Bay in 1908. Pittsburgh Phil showed up at Riley Grannon's betting station and listened as Grannon was saying, "I have $5000 that says Volante wins."

"I'll take it," Pittsburgh Phil said.

"I have five more," Grannon said.

"Take you again."

"I have five more."

"Take you again. And take five more, too."

By the time they were through the bet was $25,000. Dew Drop got off first and Volante never could catch up and after the race Grannon was paying off and asking the stranger, "What's your name?"

"George Smith," Pittsburgh Phil said.

"Smart guy," Grannon muttered to himself.

Pittsburgh Phil had a distaste for anybody who thought he was lucky. "Special knowledge is not luck," he would snap. "It is acquired by hard work and study." His other rule of life: Double your wagers when you have bookmakers in hand.

He was a cold man who, like most big gamblers, steered clear of liquor, and rarely showed emotion. Two hours before he was to die at the end of a long sickness he was stretched out in bed giving his brother Bill an order on three horses. Bill was to bet a thousand on each.

"Maybe I'm dying," Pittsburgh Phil said. "But I'll go out as I lived. Bet the money."

But for Jimmy Fitz, these were the years when he had something else to think about besides the eternal attempt to get enough on which to live.

It all had started in Maspeth when he fell. Or maybe the day in Washington when he lost weight. He really didn't remember things that clearly. All he knew was that now his back began to pain. Not an ache, either. It was a sharp, murderous pain that took up his breath and left him wracked. He could barely walk. The pain was at its worst when he was at Sheepshead Bay. He had a long walk from the stable area to the paddock, and most of them used a horse cart for the trip over. Jimmy Fitz couldn't do it. He would sooner walk miles than go through the agony of bending his back to get in or out of the wagon or a car. Not that walking was that much easier. His hip would lock on him after any amount of walking and he'd be stranded until he could work it out. If he was in a room and a heavy guy walked across it and made even the slightest vibration on the floorboards, it went through him like a knife. A sneeze or a cough became agony. At night, once he'd get himself into bed, he'd have to grab the headboard and pull himself if he wanted to move. Once seated, he became helpless. When it started, he didn't think he could live through six months with the pain. It became worse each day. He went to doctors a couple of times at the beginning, and they said something about rheumatism, gave him some medicine to take and let it go at that. He never bothered to go back. Doctors could cost you a lot of money and he didn't have any of that. He never complained. To him, it was the same as getting beat in a horse race. You took it and shut up.

This was the era where the boasts of patent medicine became nearly as outrageous as they are today. And from all parts of the stable area guys came around with bottles of stuff. Swamp Root tonic or a cure their great aunt had used for the very same kind of a pain. Or perhaps a tonic the druggist had recommended. All were guaranteed to cure the back and Jimmy Fitz said thank you to each of them, took the medicine home and put it on a shelf where it was to stay until thrown out. He never was much for taking medicine even when prescribed by a doctor. He was not about to tangle with the voodoo stuff being peddled around in those days. So he did nothing.

"The pain," he says, "went away in the queerest way. I used to sit around a place with Frank Herold and a handicapper named Billy Carmody after the races. They'd drink some beer, I'd eat ice cream. We'd gab about horses and the like and it kind of took my mind off the pain a little. Well, one night I finished the ice cream and I said I'm going to have a beer, too. So I drank it, then had another. I had maybe two, three bottles. I had some the next night, too. Then like nothing, the pain started to go away. I don't know why, but it eased up. So I kept drinking the couple of bottles of beer and before I knew it I wasn't hurting any more. I don't know whether you can give the beer any credit. If you do, make sure you put down all the guys that drinkin' ruined and killed, too. I don't want to give the booze the best of it, you know."

When the pain went away, it did not stop the backbone from gradually forcing his head downward. This was to go on little by little for years. But Jimmy Fitz didn't care about that. All he wanted to do was maneuver around horses and as long as he could do it without pain he was satisfied. But he couldn't even have this, as it developed.

8. The Backstretch

In 1907, Sunny Jim Fitzsimmons went out on his own as a trainer of horses. Anybody who had a horse or two horses or more than that and wanted them trained could come to him and he would work and hustle around and treat the horses as if they were part of his family. He was able to make a bare living doing this.

Then one afternoon in 1910, J. E. Davis, a financier, sat in his clubhouse box at Sheepshead Bay and discussed a problem with a little, sharply dressed guy named Morty Lynch. Now usually, the only problem Davis had with Morty Lynch concerned how much money he was going to give Lynch to bet on the fifth race. But a few minutes before, during lunch, Davis had written a good check which made him the owner of another race horse. He already had a few, but they were out of town with trainer Matt Brady and Davis needed somebody to take care of this new one.

"I got just the guy for you," Lynch was saying. "Little guy you probably don't even know. But I see how he takes care of what he's got. I don't think you can go wrong with him. Jimmy Fitzsimmons, his name is."

Davis said fine, we'll give him a try. Then a few minutes later Lynch hustled down to the paddock and brought this

new trainer back to Davis' box. The business took a minute
or so and then Jimmy Fitzsimmons was shaking hands with
J. E. Davis on a business deal and when he left he said
thanks to Morty Lynch. He knew Lynch just as a guy around
the race track; Mr. Fitz had done no betting business with
him. He couldn't understand why Lynch would tout a man on
him.

"I give service to clients," Lynch said. "This is a real good
fellow and I know how you handle a horse. I seen that with my
own eyes. So I do my man a favor by bringing you to him."

Nobody can remember the name of the horse any more and
you can go blind if you're crazy enough to try to look the
thing up in old records. The name isn't important, anyway.
All that really mattered was that J. E. Davis went home to
his estate on Cedar Swamp Road in swank Brookville, Long
Island, that night and during dinner he said something about
getting up a little earlier the next day because he'd like to see
if this new trainer he had taken on was as good as Morty
Lynch said he was.

He certainly was. And Davis was a man smart enough to
notice it. In business, it is attention to the fringe things that
make men rich. In horse racing, this same policy gives you a
little bit of a chance at times and Davis could see this new
one, Fitzsimmons, was a man who took care of his business—
right down the line; inspecting each horse thoroughly, wran-
gling with the feed man to get just what he wanted; in short,
doing everything that was to make him a legend in his business.

Davis was the first big money man Jimmy Fitz ever had
done business with, and he found it was not a harrowing
experience. Davis came out in the morning, looked around,
said nothing, then left for Wall Street after the workouts.

"Want anything done?" Jimmy Fitz asked him one morning.

"No," Davis said. "The only question is, am I in your way
here?"

And a few months later, Davis was having a drink with a

friend, Herbert L. Pratt, who had a little item going for him called the Standard Oil Company of New Jersey.

"Do you want to have a little fun?" Davis asked him.

"I could stand some relaxation," Pratt said.

"Then take a hundred thousand and give it to this Fitzsimmons of mine out at the track and let him buy you some yearlings and train them for you. You'll love it."

"Only a hundred thousand?" Pratt laughed.

"Sure, why not?" Davis said. "It'll give you something to do."

He was talking off-hand and half-joking, but he kept mentioning it to Pratt every time they met and finally one morning Davis came out to the barn and he called Jimmy Fitz over and said, "A friend of mine is coming out here in a day or so and I'd like you to meet him. His name is Mr. Pratt and I think he might like to race a few horses."

Which Pratt did. And after him came another friend, a man named Howard Maxwell, head of the Atlas Portland Cement Company.

It was the start. Davis, Pratt, and Maxwell didn't go in for big stables—five or six horses was the limit. But they were the first ones who showed him where the door was and how, if you kept at it, you could put your hand on the knob and turn it and open the door and walk into the big-time.

Jimmy Fitz kept this public stable even when in 1914 he was hired by a man named James F. Johnson, who owned the 34-horse Quincy Stable. It was with the Quincy Stable that the name Fitzsimmons started to become a big one in horse racing circles and the attention he drew brought him to big money. Johnson had watched him handle Davis, Pratt, and Maxwell's horses and hired him because of it.

Historically, this is how his career took a turn for the better. He trained horses that lost races, but he trained horses that won races, too, and these put the first money he ever had into his pocket. He worked for long hours to make it this way and when he wasn't working, he was home with his wife and a family that was growing.

He never lied to an owner and beat him out of money. He had no betting clients that he touted. He never told a jockey to pull a horse so he could get a high betting price on him the next time. Here and there he ran into trouble from others, but he went along as if it never happened. He was too busy working and liking people and horses to bother with much else. But these are facts from the record book, not the events that characterize him as a man. Perhaps a few incidents in his life will set the stage for an understanding of the person.

There was at this time a sportswriter on the old Brooklyn *Eagle* who made up his mind, in print, that Mr. James E. Fitzsimmons was up to no good. On several occasions, he called for action by everything this side of the militia to put a stop to the betting coups Fitzsimmons was pulling off. Mr. Fitz thought that was all right; the guy had a job to do and as long as he was shaping up for it every day it didn't matter much whether he wrote good or bad about Fitzsimmons.

"Now he's a fine writer," Mr. Fitz insisted. "Good fella, too. Knows horses better'n most of them. But he's gotten to bettin', the fool. And it's got him half nuts. Now he knows I don't bother to bet. But he just can't think right any more because of his betting, so now he's gotten himself to believe I'm doin' something with horses so I can cash a bet. It's too bad, because he's a fine fella. Well, he'll be all right soon as he learns to stay away from the betting ring."

This was the only way to live that he knew. And it was the way that was to make him a success. He always was as interested in people as he was in horses and it was the people who were to make him, just as much as any winner he ever sent out on a race track. People always were attracted to Mr. Fitz. His smile, for one thing. Mr. Fitz's smile was always a big wide thing that seems to run off his face. And he smiles whenever anybody says hello to him. You'd be surprised how many people make a point of saying hello to him just so they can see the smile. Mr. Fitz's main principle in life is to be nice to others . . . absolutely anybody who comes around. The only ornery people, horses or humans, he feels, are those who are hurting someplace. And they need care, not enemies.

One day not long ago, Mr. Fitz was sitting under a big elm tree at Belmont. A light spring rain was falling, but the leaves of the big elm stopped all but a few drops of the rain. And these few raindrops didn't touch Mr. Fitz at all. He was wearing a big tan shoot-'em-up cowboy hat with a brim wide enough to knock them dead in Dallas. You could have poured a bowl of soup into the brim and the soup wouldn't have spilled off. Because there had been a lot of security trouble in the stable area, the track wanted everybody working with horses to have identification and they had issued Mr. Fitz a big red and gold medal that said he was horse trainer Number 1 on the New York tracks. He was proud of the medal and he wore it right out on his jacket lapel. It was a good thing to have, he was telling the people around him, because now all the guards at the race track would know he was a horse trainer and not some guy sneaking around to dope horses.

Across from him, Johnny Longden came out of the red brick building where the jockeys get dressed. Longden is a little man of fifty-one who is bald, speaks in a high voice, and has enough money to be a bank. He was looking around for people he knew because this was the first time he had been out of California to ride a horse in ten years. At fifty-one, Longden still is one of the great riders in the world. When he breaks a leg or some other bone in a fall during a race, people always say this will finally make him quit. Longden says nothing. He has the leg put in a cast and when the cast comes off a riding boot goes on and Longden goes up on five horses the next day. Johnny had on yellow silks on this day and he walked up to talk to his wife, a tall blond woman who was standing in front of the jockey's quarters. Longden looked across and saw Mr. Fitz, then he took his wife by the arm and brought her over to the old man.

"Mr. Fitz," he said, "I was just telling my wife a few weeks ago, 'Let's call up Mr. Fitz and go back East and ride out the summer for him and then we'll call it quits.' I figured as long as I started with you, I might as well finish in the same place."

"You started with him?" Longden was asked.

"Here's the man that made me. You know, Mr. Fitz, I can remember you coming up to me at Hialeah. That was 1937 but I remember it like it was just a few days ago. You came up and asked me if I wanted to ride for you. You had a lot of trouble getting me to say yes, didn't you?" Longden laughed.

"Well, I saw that you were a real good one."

"I don't know what would have happened with me if you didn't come around. I wasn't doin' much of anything."

"Oh, you would have made it the same way you did. Just would have taken you a little more time maybe."

"I don't know about that, Mr. Fitz. I didn't know much about riding until I got with you. Mightn't have learned it, either."

"Ahhhhh," Mr. Fitz said. He waved his hand at Longden.

"You look wonderful," Longden's wife said.

"I'm fine. Just lost some of my speed, that's all."

Everybody laughed, and then Longden went back to the jockey's room.

"What did you do to make this guy?" Mr. Fitz was asked.

"Just watched him ride, that's all. And don't say I made him. You can't say that at all. He was ridin' there probably as good as he ever did, but he wasn't on winners so nobody noticed him much. But I could see he was a crackerjack. I asked him to come to work for me. That's all I did. Couldn't do much else. He did the ridin' himself. You can see that by the record. He's fifty-one now. Still rides better'n all them fellas on the Coast. He's a wonder."

Later in the day, Longden was talking about this and he said he didn't think Mr. Fitz was telling it exactly the way it happened.

"The man taught me an awful lot of things about riding

horses," he was saying. "No, I don't think I could give you a specific thing just now. I mean, we're just standin' here talking and Mr. Fitz, he showed me just about the whole business. So for me to pick out one thing would be hard. You could put down that he made me."

"He doesn't think so."

"Well, you don't think he sits out there and says 'I did this for this man' and 'I did that for that man.' He's got more on his mind than things like this. That's why he's Mr. Fitz.

"I'll tell you," he said. "I can still hear him saying one thing to me. 'A good jockey don't need orders, a bad jockey forgets them.' First thing he told me."

"Lot of years," Longden said. "Seems I been riding forever. I guess Mr. Fitz can tell you why I'm still going."

"He'll say he didn't do a thing."

"That's his style."

It is a great style for a guy to have. And Mr. Fitz never went back on it. Check over his career and look into the way he did things and you see the man came with class. Go back into the years when he was starting to make it and you see evidence of it all over.

In August of 1914, for one thing, Quincy Stable was being trained by Steve Lawlor and the best horse in the barn was a two-year-old named Trojan who was training up to the rich Futurity like a good thing. The Futurity was at Saratoga that year and it was worth $16,000 to the winner, $1600 of this to the trainer. In 1914 you could get off the nut for a long time on $1600.

The Quincy Stable's owner, James F. Johnson, was a straight old Brooklyn Irishman who was in the sugar weighing business. He wanted to hire Mr. Fitz as his trainer. "I want you to take the horses right here," he told Mr. Fitz.

"Now what about Trojan?" Mr. Fitz said.

"He's part of the stable. You take him," Johnson said.

"I don't think so," Mr. Fitz said. "I better take Trojan when

we get back down to New York. Lawlor's got him coming
along fine for the Futurity and I don't want to do anything
that might upset the horse. Looks like he might win the race.
Lawlor probably knows things about the horse I don't and I'd
only mess it up. You better leave him as he is."

Johnson let it stand that way and ten days later Trojan
busted around the last turn on top and won the Futurity and
Lawlor got his $1600. That was the way Mr. Fitz wanted it.

Then there was an afternoon when Edward Heffner, a
trainer, was in trouble with a horse called Dolan. He had
gotten Dolan for $4000 in a claiming race and he was having
trouble because the horse wouldn't run straight. The horse
kept sidling instead of following his nose and Heffner was
a little nervous, because $4000 was awful good money to have
in a horse that wouldn't run.

One morning, when Dolan was causing all kinds of trouble
on the track at Aqueduct, Mr. Fitz was watching and he told
Heffner he might have an idea for a different rigging of the
horse's tack that would stop Dolan from messing up. Later
that morning, Frank Herold came into Heffner's barn with
some of Mr. Fitz's rigging.

"He says to use this," Herold said. "And he's got a pony you
can use to lead the horse and calm him down." The stable
pony was sent over on loan a little while after.

Two weeks later, Heffner had Dolan running straight, and
fast, too, and the horse was entered in a race at Aqueduct
which listed Filemaker, trained by J. Fitzsimmons, as another
entry.

"Look out for me this time," Heffner told Mr. Fitz. "I got
my horse to running good."

Mr. Fitz got a kick out of it. Two days later, Dolan won
the race, with Filemaker running second, and Mr. Fitz didn't
like that so much, but if you're going to lose, that's the
way he will lose them. And if Heffner had run into any trouble
with the horse the day after that, Mr. Fitz would have taken

a look and helped him again if he could. And if anybody would have asked him what he had done for Dolan he would have said nothing, just loaned his trainer some equipment, that's all; and didn't the horse run a good race the other day?

These are just a couple of things about the man. They aren't the great big things that you could make speeches about. But they're the kind of things Mr. Fitz goes in for. And they all come under the heading of a word which is very misused as a rule. If the word were used properly, you'd rarely see it in print. The word is charity. It doesn't mean a handout. It means you have some class with other human beings.

When you look at it, Mr. Fitz's disposition could come from self-preservation as much as anything else. He lived with so many people during his life that it was either be nice or be dead from arguing. Anybody knows that large Irish families, when placed under one roof, usually tear one another to bits. Now the Fitzsimmons family reached battalion strength, less one company perhaps, when Mr. Fitz came back to Sheepshead Bay for good from Torresdale, in 1905. Yet the roster shows they never lost a man as a result of this togetherness, which under the Fitzsimmons way of life is like the rush hour. And Mr. Fitz even insists, vehemently, too, that police never were summoned even once to break up out-of-hand kitchen table discussions. This is undoubtedly a record for the Irish in North America. Anthropologists can tell you that angry Sicilians, even if they are on red wine, are not as dangerous as Irish people at a kitchen table.

When Mr. Fitz came back to Sheepshead Bay he moved into a place called the Old Homestead, a big and even then ancient house which had served as General Howe's headquarters while he was getting ready for the Battle of Long Island. The beams had been hand hewn, with wooden pegs used instead of nails, and ax marks, put there by colonial housebuilders, could be seen throughout the place. More important, it had room. For Mr. Fitz came with his wife, four children, Frank Herold, Fish Tappen, Jockey Joe McCahey, and five stablehands. The house was already occupied by his sisters Nora and Kate and brothers Steve, George, and Tom. The number of children, of course, was not to remain static. There was also a pony named Sonny, who came into the kitchen between swings of the door and stole food. Also, off and on, such visitors as Johnny Burton, the dancing school man from Trenton, who had two non-business interests in life: the couple of race horses he owned and an amazing collection of the best trap-door union suits a man could ever want to have. Burton spent his working time teaching people how to stay off each other's feet while shuffling around with a cracking Texas Tommie. But every chance he got he'd pack up and maneuver around the race tracks with Mr. Fitz. Burton learned from the start that a man on a race track had to move extra quick or he'd wind up doing the two-step with bill collectors. He also learned that when eating in the stable area it was best to keep that fork going like a metronome.

There was one Friday meal, back at a place called the Eagle track, outside of Philadelphia, when Frank Herold came up with a piece of hambone and Burton began to scrape the meat from the knuckles to give him something remotely resembling a dinner of fried ham and eggs. While Burton was working on the knuckles, Miller, an old cook and general utility man who was around the stable, got interested. Miller spent most of his time getting on the good side of everybody. His main pitch was insisting that he was a Catholic. He figured this would set him up pretty good with Mr. Fitz. But the ham was making his position difficult. He kept giving it a look, then finally decided to make a bid for it.

"Mr. Johnny," Miller said, "ain't I going to get some of that ham?"

Burton felt safe as a baby. "You're a Catholic," he said, "I can't let you have any meat on Friday."

"Now Mr. Johnny," Miller said, "you know I a liar."

The most important people at the Old Homestead were the

horses. They were cheap as horses go and some of them were broken down, but they were horses people had given to Mr. Fitz and that meant they were going to be treated as if they were part of the family. When he started on his own after working for Colonel Morrell in Torresdale, Mr. Fitz had horses from people like Burton and Barney Flynn, a New York saloon-keeper who looked like a bishop but had a bung-starter right hand that was famous along the Bowery. A betting commissioner named Roxy Angarola gave Mr. Fitz his horses. So did Christy Sullivan of the Sullivans of Tammany Hall. And a man named Richard Johnson, who at one time was the warden of Sing Sing prison.

The horses at first were kept in a barn behind the Old Homestead and as more were taken on they were put in other barns around the neighborhood. Mr. Fitz was in no position to get stable space from the Sheepshead or Gravesend or Brighton tracks, which had room only for the big recognized outfits. At this time, streams crisscrossed Sheepshead Bay— they long since have been diverted and filled up to make way for big apartment houses—and Mr. Fitz and Herold and Fish had to build bridges over them to get the horses from the various barns to the race track.

Bob Shanahan, who rubbed the Fitzsimmons horses, came up with the lumber to build the bridges. Nobody asked him where it came from. In fact, nobody questioned anything Shanahan did. For some reason, he liked to bet on jumping races and would walk through flames to get to one of them. One afternoon, for example, Shanahan was still working on his horses at the Old Homestead when he found he had about 35 minutes to make it to the Gravesend track and get his bet down on the jumping race. He put on a clean shirt and started to leave when somebody stopped him and said he looked a bit seedy because he hadn't shaved that day.

Shanahan grabbed a sharp knife and a piece of soap and began to walk as fast as his legs would carry him on the three-mile walk to the track. While he was walking, he would spit on the soap, rub the soap against his jowls to produce the hint of lather, then hack away at the whiskers with the knife. When he began to work at the Adam's apple with the knife, anybody looking out the front window figured he was witnessing a suicide attempt.

The horses usually came with something wrong with them, but they were getting high class care and this was something people around the race track started to notice. Mr. Fitz took cripples and worked them into running order so often that people on the track talked about it. Some of them even helped. John E. Madden, the Kentucky breeder, gave him a filly called Miss Angie—"Pay me if you win, I like the way you do a day's work" Madden said—and Mr. Fitz won a couple of races with her and Madden had his money. Arthur B. Hancock, Sr., another breeder, gave Mr. Fitz a filly under the same arrangement—the horse was named Edith F. after his latest addition to the family, a daughter. Edith F. won races, Hancock got his money and more people began to talk about this Fitzsimmons. Then came Davis and Pratt and a regular stable at the track and things looked good.

At this time, just when everything seemed to be starting to turn for Jimmy Fitz, piety became a tremendous issue in New York. Religious fanatics crept out of the woodwork, and their quick-talking, Bible-quoting speeches began to influence legislative thinking, con newspaper editors, and excite the people. Committees for Law and Order popped up everywhere. Their target was racing at first, then drinking.

Then, in 1910, the lawmakers, with the aid of Governor Charles Evans Hughes, said they thought betting was immoral. The sport of horse racing was banned in New York.

Now to appreciate what happened at this time, you've got to know something about gambling in general and race track betting in particular. Since all gambling is done by people, any knowledge is at best inexact. However, you can be certain that any kind of gambling, race track betting included, can become a terrible disease. Right along with alcoholism. As a means of creating trouble, gambling, of course, runs a terrible second to sex, but it is most certainly a lot easier to ban. Although a ban does not mean betting on horses stops. This is something which can never be stopped because there always is a set of people who like to bet on horses and they will walk on broken bottles to get a bet in. England has recognized this for some time now and has horse betting legalized all over the place. Since this has the faint odor of common sense about it, we should not expect this country to follow suit for some time.

As for the morals of it all, you can get an idea by looking at the different classes of people in this country who gamble. There is, first, the degenerate. He will bet the baby's milk money, let his wife go shoeless and lose his self-respect at the drop of a dollar. He is a sick man. Has been from the time he was six or seven years old, probably. He'll bet on horses. If you close them up, he'll shoot crap in an alley. Stop that and he'll play cards in a gas station. He will contrive, one way or the other, to get rid of his money if he has to wind up betting on bus numbers. It doesn't matter whether you have a race track open or not. The degenerate gambler will get rid of it all.

Then you have the guy or woman who gets a kick out of betting, goes to the track figuring to lose a few dollars and proceeds to do so while having a wonderful time. This type makes up the overwhelming majority of people who attend horse races in this country. They bet because they happen to like it. Now this is the type the reformers claim is put upon by race tracks. The tracks, they say, reach out and grab these people and pull them in, then take the rent money from them. Rent money most certainly does get blown at the track, many times by these normally sensible pleasure bettors. They blow the rent almost as much as it is blown by normally sensible pleasure bettors chancing it on baseball or professional football, the two most gambled-on sports in the entire world.

But on the whole, people who go to the races do not bet over their heads. They simply walk around, chew on a sandwich perhaps, read a program or form sheet until the eyes blur, then talk excitedly the rest of the day about a sure thing they know is about to come off in the fifth. They bet the race and lose. They wouldn't bet any more than they planned to if you twisted their arm. They go home tired—and ready to save for the next time. There is no more wrong in this than there is sitting home in the living room.

The legislators in New York State felt they had the answer to a great, steaming demon of an evil when, in 1908, they passed the Perkins-Agnew bill, which made any effort at wagering on horse race illegal.

The bookmakers, however, had an answer to that. They came up with what they called "oral betting." You went up to a bookmaker, told him what you wanted to bet, and that was it. The book, his hand thrust into his pants pocket, merely nodded. He was writing the bet down inside his pocket as clearly as if it were typewritten. Such as Izzy Hamm, and Big Sol Lichenstein, became know as "Memory Brokers." Under an interpretation, this was ruled legal.

Governor Hughes moved to close this gap. He had a bill introduced which would jail anybody connected with the track, from such as August Belmont on down, if gambling laws were violated. It was introduced as the Hart-Agnew bill and the vote was a tie. On April 23, 1910, the legislature adjourned. In the meantime a Republican legislator from the Niagara Falls part of the state died. Hughes appeared for a special election to replace him and stumped for a guy he knew would back his anti-betting bill. This accomplished, he called a special session of the legislature on May 11 to vote on the anti-betting bill. Again it looked like a tie—the track interests had grabbed a guy, too—until the doors in the chamber opened and they brought in one Otto Foelker, a Republican from Brooklyn who had just had his appendix removed. He was on a stretcher. Foelker was a thick-headed Dutchman with colossal nerve—he wasn't even a citizen, therefore was holding office illegally. But with his heart filled with piety, he voted against the bill and racing now was illegal in New York State by a 26–25 vote.

While he was governor, Hughes did a job on racing. And Mr. Fitz found himself once more on the road, traveling with horses while his wife and children followed by train and sometimes he had to wonder why he didn't take the job of running a trolley car in Philadephia.

9. Heading for the Top

With New York in the hands of people who said they were close to God, the racing crowd had to scatter. Some went to Europe to make a living, a few of the horsemen stayed around New York and helped run hunt meets at private clubs on Long Island which millionaire sportsmen like Davis backed to keep the game alive. Jimmy Fitz, having taken to the road again, arrived at Moncrief Park, Jacksonville, Florida, in 1912, with eight or nine horses, four children, no money, and a little bit of Irish hope that he'd get some.

The day he shipped in, he was around the stable area and ran into Snapper Garrison, the jockey, who was walking along with Colonel Phillip T. Chinn of Lexington, Kentucky, Juarez, Mexico, and any other such promising place.

"How're your horses?" Garrison said.

"Fine," Mr. Fitz said.

"Well, tell you what I'm going to do," Garrison said. "I know you don't have much money. So I'm going to go out and buy you a whole mess of padlocks and you can lock in your horses so's nothin' happens to them. No sense runnin' them. Colonel Phil T. Chinn here, he has this game by the a-double-s."

The colonel beamed. He then hustled away. He seemed to have the horses to blanket the meeting all right, but the trouble

165

was he did not know who owned them at the moment. Chinn owed the slight matter of $4000 to Izzy Hamm, a bookmaker. Now Hamm had extensive connections with the sheriff's office, and as he saw it, the debt could be most easily resolved if the sheriff would help him foreclose on Chinn's horses the next day. But Chinn had an angle or two going for him at Moncrief Park. As did nearly everybody else on the grounds, Mr. Fitz had to learn.

That night, Chinn had dinner with Charles White, a New York bookmaker, and during their little talk Chinn mapped out a quite workable plan for a successful betting operation. White loved it.

"I'd also like to get the use of four thousand until I can get my runners in action," Mr. Chinn said.

White said he knew where to get it. He walked out of the hotel dining room, stalked into the lobby, grabbed Izzy Hamm and asked for a short-term character loan in that amount. For an old friend and fellow bookmaker, Hamm dug down and came up with it. White said thank you and walked away. Some seconds later, Chinn was in the lobby flashing the money and calling out, "Izzy, you come over here. I'm going to straighten this situation out." Hamm became half-smart about now and let out a scream. They usually do. He also came down with laryngitis by the time he was through handling bets on what was to follow.

Now Moncrief Park was run by a man named Curly Brown who, his grandmother always said, was thoroughly honest. Brown also came with the courage of a bear and a loaded .45 in his pocket. He was the official starter at the track and for a time had to take the insults of irate bettors because of his work. One of them arrived in Brown's office one day and pointed a gun at Curly. He started to make a speech about what was going to happen. Brown, thoroughly bored, got up from his desk, walked up to the guy and then threw him out the window, gun and all.

With stories such as this being spread around, complaints

about Brown's work grew dim and soon hardly anybody seemed surprised, or would say much more than hello, when Brown would be seen around the betting ring before a race. This was fairly unorthodox behavior for a starter. As was one of his more flamboyant starts. When the race went off, one horse took a stride forward, then wheeled and ran straight back toward the barn. Brown promptly had the field recalled. He sent them off twice more before he let it stick and the race be run. The horse which had tried to run away the first time, and an animal for which Brown seemed to have more than normal love, broke well on top the second time. This was, said people who knew about the gun in Brown's pocket, merely a coincidence.

If you are around the huge, orderly business that racing is today, you have to wonder if a man like Brown ever existed. But exist he did, and for a good reason. Men of the caliber of a J. E. Davis had been, by law, forced to limit their racing activities to a few hunt meets at such places as the Piping Rock Club on Long Island. For somebody like Fitzsimmons, whose life was committed to being with horses, this situation left him at a place where a Curly Brown would be in charge.

Not that he is ever going to complain about it. With absolute stubbornness, he rails if you sit down and say, "Now tell me about how this guy Brown robbed you."

"I don't know that," he will snap. "And neither do you. There was racing there and I made my living at it and that's all that I know or ever knew about it. I don't know the first thing about anything he did. And don't you start having me say anything about racing except how good it's been for all of us."

Which is, of course, the way of the stand-up guy.

The facts, however, would disturb lesser people. When Jimmy Fitz sent out a horse called Via Octavio at Moncrief, there was trouble over the race. Joe McCahey, a little-faced kid out of Philadelphia, was on the horse. He was, as records proved afterward, as fine a lightweight jock as they had in the business, and he never did a thing wrong in his life. Aboard Via Octavio, he got tucked into a pocket, couldn't get out of it and lost the race. These things happen every day, but the minute the race was over, Judge George Murphy solemnly called McCahey to the stewards' stand. Murphy was an old, proud-looking man who would scuttle the Atlantic Fleet. He told McCahey that he was going to be suspended for pulling Via Octavio. Curly Brown came up to the stand and seemed considerably agitated.

"We're going to rule this kid off," Brown told Fitzsimmons a few minutes later. "We think he pulled the horse. Now if you say so, too, we'll have a good case."

Brown most certainly did not say that any agreement by Fitzsimmons would be of benefit to Brown when he met with his bookmakers later and discussed the money he had put down on Via Octavio. But he did get mad when Jimmy Fitz refused to fault McCahey's dead-level ride. McCahey was told to pack up and get off the track and for a few days Moncrief Park refused any entries from trainer J. Fitzsimmons. When he did get horses in, he did all right and things were moving along at a good clip when the racing secretary came to him one morning and asked if Royal Captive, who had just lost a race a couple of days before, could be entered in the race that day as a favor. The secretary hadn't been able to fill the event and needed some help. He got it from Fitzsimmons. The trouble was, he got too much help. Royal Captive, an outsider in the betting, went to the post and won the race and Curly Brown and Judge Murphy blew their tops again. They didn't like an upset at times.

When the meeting ended, and Jimmy Fitz was shipping North, with money in his pocket to do it with, too, the great Colonel Chinn came around to see him.

The meeting, for Colonel Chinn, had been a disaster. He tried to cash a bet or two, was whacked out of the box, then his horses started to come up hurt. The horses didn't complain, but the bookmakers and bill collectors did and Jacksonville was not Chinn's idea of paradise at the moment.

"You 'member when we first got here I told you I had this thing by the tail down here?" Chinn said. "Well, let me tell you. Looks like right now the only man who got anything by the tail is the sheriff. And the one he's got is me."

In 1912, the ban on racing was repealed and Mr. Fitz came back to New York and started to build his career again. And now you could see he was not going to miss. It was all the same—a cheap horse, a lot of work on the cheap horse and then just enough money to pay the bills. But during all of this, one thing was becoming apparent to everybody who saw him working and succeeding with everything he was given.

"He has," they said, "an eye for a horse." This is one of the oldest of the Irish expressions. There is no casual meaning to it because in the old country, where it comes from, thorough-bred horses are a serious business. And only a few men are accepted as knowing much about these animals. They said it about Mr. Fitz.

They also began to realize that Mr. Fitz had an eye for the right way of doing things, too. He had been rummaging around the country for several years and he was not a con-sistent churchgoer. On most Sundays, digging up food was the main project and that did not leave much time for scouting around the countryside for a church—if there was one to be found. But religion is a way of life, not just a Sunday business, and it includes things like being honest, which is Mr. Fitz's hole card.

Joe McCahey, the little jockey Mr. Fitz brought up, was one who knew it. McCahey was a fine lightweight rider who had a deep trust in God, and as many gold certificates as he could get his paws on. Such things as the usual paper money, most human beings, and any and all occasions which required money to be spent were not for McCahey. It was different if it was Mr. Fitz. Then, Joe never had a question. He'd do anything, as long as he was doing it with Mr. Fitz. But with anybody else, Joe was a little suspicious.

He roomed with Frank Herold and the first night the two

put up together, McCahey declared the hand. He took a wad of folded gold certificates out of his pocket—he was riding well and was the only one with any money—and handed them to Herold.

"Put this under your pillow and sleep on it for me," McCahey said.

"Why don't you do it yourself?" Frank asked.

"Because if I sleep on it and you put your hand in during the night and take some of the money off me, you can say you don't know nothing about it. You could say some thief come in here while we both was asleep. But if you got it under your pillow then you won't take it because you know I wouldn't believe any story you tell me in the morning. Take the money. It's safer for me like this."

McCahey went to bed and slept like a firedog. Herold spent most of the night trying to figure out how this little guy next to him was able to arrive at that kind of logic.

Herold soon found out he had to spend a lot of time thinking around McCahey. The little jockey was adept at such things as having no change when it came to paying for a trolley car ride and making sure he was alone when it was time to eat in a restaurant so he wouldn't be faced with the prospects of paying for somebody else. McCahey bought a car for the Saratoga season one summer, but after paying the gas and oil bills for it a few times, he gave it to Herold for the rest of the season. By his strange logic, he figured he was saving money.

With Mr. Fitz, he went the other way. By 1913, the scrapping had started to pay off, and Mr. Fitz wanted to build a house in Sheepshead Bay. He was shy $8000 and things like bank loans and mortgages were something he didn't think much about. He asked McCahey about the money. Joe didn't bother with formalities. He came up with the $8000 in gold certificates. It was always gold notes with McCahey; he spent most of his non-riding hours going around exchanging paper for them because he did not trust normal currency. Yet McCahey, who would not spend a quarter to see an earthquake, didn't even think about giving Mr. Fitz $8000. He just started to count it out.

McCahey was paid off in 1914 when Mr. Fitz got lucky with a horse named Rosseaux. The horse was running at old Empire City track in Yonkers, New York, and a fellow named Bud May claimed him for $1700 from a friend of Mr. Fitz's, Bob McKeever.

After the horse was claimed, Mr. Fitz talked to May, who said he'd resell the horse for a $200 profit. Mr. Fitz liked the horse, and knew he could do something with it. But under his code he had to tell McKeever, the original owner, about it first.

"I know you liked the horse," Mr. Fitz told him. "You can get it back for a $200 profit."

McKeever said he'd rather forget about it, so Mr. Fitz got Johnson, the prison warden, to put up the money for the horse. Then he took Rosseaux in hand and the mare started winning races, good races, too, and presently a sign appeared over Mr. Fitz's new house at 1174 Sheepshead Bay Road. THE ROSSEAUX, it read.

The Rosseaux, with the Fitzsimmons family living in it, resembled a boardinghouse, particularly in the summers when the family would line the long front porch. What with the sign and the number of people on the premises, anybody in the neighborhood looking for a room during the racing season would come up the walk, suitcase in hand, and ask what the rates were. When they were told it was not a rooming house they would walk off muttering, thinking they were being turned down on appearance.

McCahey took on weight and became sick and had to leave racing. He died in North Carolina at the age of twenty-seven. He left $52,000 in gold certificates and named Fitzsimmons as executor of the will. This didn't seem to bother his mother at all. When her son's body was shipped to her house in Philadelphia, the casket almost completely filled the living room and visitors would find her sitting in the room and shaking her head as she looked at her son.

"I can't understand why they didn't send Joe's overcoat up with him," she said.

By 1914, when Mr. Fitz went with James Johnson and his Quincy Stable, everybody on the race track knew what he was like and what he could do and the only question was just how high he could go. Everybody thought it would be very high. And everybody means a lot of people because they were starting to come around Mr. Fitz now and get a taste of his warmth and when they went away they felt as if they had a friend they were going to keep for a long time. And they made sure to come again and to see him smile and talk, just as people would every day for the next forty-six years.

The newspaper writers were part of the crowd. It used to be J. Fitzsimmons in agate type next to a horse he rode or in the charts if he trained a winner. But now it was Jimmy Fitzsimmons in stories and Fitz and Fitzsimmons and Jim Fitzsimmons in 36- and 48-point headlines and finally one day George Daley of the *World* started his story by saying: "Jimmy Fitzsimmons—Sunny Jim they ought to call him because of a disposition that ever makes for a happy smile—had three good ones at Jamaica yesterday." The copyreader had a two-column head to put over the story, and he used "Sunny Jim" in the head and it was the name that was to stick. It was in nearly everybody's stories after that. And there were plenty of them. The sportswriters read as if they were writing of an old friend and the people who read papers started to talk about him and as Mr. Fitz started to knock them dead with winners around New York tracks, the sports world opened for him.

Everything became like the afternoon at Empire City when Jack Kearns, the great fight manager, came into the paddock with a dark-haired, murderous kid from Manassa, Colorado, and as they walked, Kearns was telling this fighter of his, "Hype Igoe introduces me to a terrific guy before. We'll go over and say hello. You'll love the guy."

Then Kearns came over to Mr. Fitz and introduced his fighter, Jack Dempsey.

Mr. Fitz stepped away from Dempsey and looked him over from hocks to head, as if he were the four horse in the next race.

"Look at him," Mr. Fitz said. "Built for speed. Oh, you can see that. Don't have to know much to see you're built for speed, boy."

Dempsey and Kearns stayed around and talked with Mr. Fitz and soon there was a crowd in a circle around them, laughing and listening to the talk. It was just a little thing that happened during a day at the races, but they put it all in the papers the next day, all about how the champ and Sunny Jim talked at the track. It got to be like this every day.

Mr. Fitz loved it. Not the stories. They meant nothing. Nor did it matter much that it was a big-name personality who was around to see him. What Mr. Fitz loved was simply that there were lots of people around. There would be the steady ones, Fish and Herold and the horse owners and jockeys and other people in the business. Now, to make it better, there were others. Whether they were reporters or show-business names or milk-delivery men was not important. Just so long as they came.

He was stepping into the world of sports for the first time, but he was different. It can be, this thing called sports, like show business. The winner finds he is a national figure and is included in a fast-moving, publicity-conscious, name-dropping circle that attracts hangers-on and well-wishers and produces as many megalomaniacs per headline as any movie studio. But Mr. Fitz never noticed he was entering this. He was surprised when strangers would know his name, just as surprised as he is forty-six years later. He never thought much about what they said about him in the newspapers. The suspicion is he has always liked the pictures a little bit more, although when he first started to pose for photographers he tried a little too hard and, particularly when he wore a hat, came out looking like a guy being booked for burglary. Later on, when he took back off the pace a little and relaxed, he became perhaps the best-photographed subject in sports. Even this is something which did not change him. He liked the picture posing and made sure to see them when they were printed, but never thought of them as being significant of anything except a little fun between trying to figure out what he could do for horses that were hurting.

"Did you ever think that you were on your way to being important?" Mr. Fitz was asked once when he was talking about these years.

"Important?" The hand made that little waving motion in front of him. "I never was important. Never will be. Get that important stuff right out of your head. That's nonsense."

This outlook is part of his success. An important part.

"Fitzsimmons is one of the characters of the race track," a guy on the New York *Sun* wrote. "To begin with, he wears suspenders. He doesn't bother about whether or not there are any creases in his trousers, either, and on hot days he takes his coat off and carries it around under his arm. He wouldn't feel comfortable in a silk shirt, and he's not particular about the color effect when it comes to neckties. Fitz is just a horse trainer. He has no connection with betting cliques, and any time he bets more than $5 on a horse, the horse is 'in.' One of these days some rich man is going to put Jimmy Fitzsimmons in charge of a regular stable, and then let all the Jimmy Rowes, Walter Jenningses, Tom Healeys and Sam Hildreths look to their laurels."

In those days, incidentally, Mr. Fitz always was able to have more fun with the mob around him in the paddock when he didn't look so smart with a horse than when he would have some good winners popping home.

One afternoon at Jamaica, Mr. Fitz was around telling everybody that his horse Liola couldn't be worse than third in the next race.

"You can step right out with this one, boys," he was saying.

174

"Go heavy. I'm unbucklin' my belt myself. We'll have them all in trouble on this one."

Liola took the track and ran as if she owed the chiropractor money. She was dead last all the way around and at the eight pole a little black bulldog darted out from the infield, took the track near Liola, skipped home well ahead of the horse, then disappeared back into the infield.

"I told you I wasn't so smart," he said to the mob after the race. He was delighted when the papers made a big thing out of the bulldog beating his sure-thing home.

On another occasion he was in the middle of a discussion about the buying of yearlings and since he was considered to be quite a hand at this, he was asked about it. Mr. Fitz gave his views on the subject and then, making sure everybody was listening, he said he knew all there was to know about yearlings.

"Why, a few months ago I bought a yearling by Spanish Prince out of a very high-class broodmare," he said. "A real corker."

"How does he look now?" he was asked. "What are you doing with him?"

"I don't know. Sold him for $50 because the minute we started to put him in training you could see he never would get to the races."

He liked telling that story.

Johnson, the Quincy Stable owner, was not a rich man compared to the Whitneys and Belmonts and others in racing. But he had a sugar weighing business on Wall Street which gave him enough income to own horses and bet on them pretty good whenever he had a spot. In the process of keeping alive in an expensive game, Johnson bought and sold horses, looked to cash a bet here and there as well as ride with the normal fortunes and misfortunes which would hit his horses when they ran for money.

It didn't matter to Johnson that Fitzsimmons was a non-bettor. He was a man who no more would have thought of asking Fitzsimmons to do something than the trainer would think of offering to do it. Johnson also was a man who had a lot of trouble getting his horses to go off at a decent price. He had a habit, it seems, of going around to his friends and making sure they were not risking their money when one of his horses was entered in a race that seemed too tough. When a spot to risk a bet would come up, Johnson would make a big thing of telling it to nobody except the first two or three or four people he would bunk into. As a rule, a word given secretly to the first four people you meet at a race track rarely reaches more than 10,000 others. Johnson continually would walk into the betting ring after advising his few friends and then explode when it would become apparent half of America was betting his horse.

"Somebody's talking," he would howl.

As for his trainer, Johnson was certain he was getting the best of it. He'd do the betting and let Fitzsimmons do the training. It turned out well.

The way it worked with the horse Captain Alcock shows this. Johnson bought the horse for $7900, turned him over to Fitzsimmons and then thought about shooting himself when he watched the horse in his first couple of starts in Quincy Stable colors. The race would start and Captain Alcock would come out of the gate in a cute, mincy little stride that would leave him five lengths out of it before things even started.

Mr. Fitz decided to take the horse to the starting gate one morning for a little schooling in how to break out of there fast and pay a few bills. The exercise boy would yelp, give the Captain a good bang on the fanny to excite him, then start pumping with his arms. Each time, the Captain reacted to all this in identical fashion. He would make a number of delicate movements, which would break anybody who had to feed him or bet on him, then settle into a clean stride which, in a race, would get him a sixth or, if he was extra good, fifth.

This went on for several days. After his morning workouts, the Captain would return to the barn and eat like a champion. "The horse could break Wall Street," Johnson said after catching one such workout and feeding.

To Mr. Fitz, it was just another case of a horse not doing what he was born to do. This meant there was something physically wrong with the animal. Everybody else said it was orneriness, but this is something Mr. Fitz doesn't believe exists in people and he got the Captain back in the barn and began to work on him. First the legs. Then the back. Then the throat and mouth. Then the horse would be walked and the moves would be watched carefully. It took time, but there is always time to be spent on a horse that is hurting someplace, and cold winters in New Jersey and the summers of hunger in Maryland paid off now because if there was one thing this man knew it was what to do with an unsound horse. It turned out, after all the probing, to be the Captain's kidneys. Mr. Fitz piled thick blankets on the Captain until it looked like the horse wouldn't be able to stand with all the weight on his back. The Captain began to sweat and lather and Mr. Fitz kept piling the blankets on and finally one morning at Aqueduct they broke the Captain from the gate and with no pain causing him to flinch when he started to move, the horse slammed out of the gate.

Mr. Fitz put him in a race at Saratoga and the charts showed the Captain finishing fifth, but anybody who saw the race knew he broke well. He was beaten only a couple of lengths for all of it and he was the fastest horse on the track at the finish.

"He needed the race," Mr. Fitz said after it. "We'll run him back in New York and he should be right up there. He's a fine horse now."

The horse was put in a race at Belmont Park and the bookmakers listed him as 70-1. "Price is way out of line," Mr. Fitz was saying in the paddock before the race. "They see he was out of the money last time, but what they don't know is how well he ran. I think he should be one of the favorites."

Nobody believed him and the price stayed there. Which was fine with Johnson. His trainer had done the job for which he was hired. Now Johnson was going to take care of his interests. While his trainer was in the paddock without a nickel riding on the horse and only caring that patience with the Captain had made him a useful animal, Johnson was in the clubhouse moving on the bookmakers. At 70–1, he was going to take a little piece of this. The bookmakers obliged him and then, a few minutes later, they were placing one bill on top of the other to form a bundle of $70,000 to give their client, Mr. Johnson. While they counted, Captain Alcock, with Joe Mooney leaning forward and patting him on the neck, was loping toward the winner's circle. The horse had run his race, as Mr. Fitz told everybody he would. Johnson was delighted. It was a terrific score. Mr. Fitz was delighted. He had helped a horse.

The gentleman from the Brooklyn *Eagle* watched the race from the press stand and he didn't like it at all.

"Thief," he muttered when the Captain took the lead at the eight pole and came down a winner. "Terrible thief," he muttered when the Captain came to the winner's circle. "Murderer," he screamed when he heard about Johnson's big score.

That night, the gentleman from the *Eagle* got to a typewriter in the sports department of his paper and he was so anxious to go to work on Fitzsimmons, he didn't know which key to hit first. In those days, libel was something papers printed as a matter of policy. It was open house for the kind known as a typewriter tough guy. It is amazing how little in the way of guts it takes to sit down at a typewriter and try to do a job on somebody. You can be the most frightened person on earth, but left alone at a typewriter and with an outlet to print what you're writing, you can be tougher than Khrushchev. So on this soft September evening, he sat in the *Eagle* sports department and he was the champ. His typewriter jumped up and down and he wrote with anger.

The next day's paper carried an eight-column line on the sports page which read:

FITZSIMMONS NOTORIOUS IN AND OUTER

The one-column head reading out from the line said:

QUINCY STABLE TRAINER
NOTED AS ONE OF RANKEST
FORM ADHERENTS
Horses Invariably Cause Form
Upsets—Hidden Influences
Hold Him Up
Recent Episode Unbearable

The story, a corker, was filled with such as:

"The most glaring spectacle of slipping it over on the public . . . what this Fitzsimmons person does under the watchful eye and protection of the Jockey Club . . . this brazen perpetration to get the money has been allowed to go unnoticed . . . it was purely a piece of sharp practice by this form flip-flapper to make a killing . . ."

Mr. Fitz felt badly for the gentleman.

Mr. Fitz was moving to the top now, toward days when the dice would nearly always come up seven. And he was building this career in a period of racing that is always considered the best years the sport ever had. It was a time when they ran only six races a day on a four-day week and winters were spent resting horses and conditioning them properly for the next season, not racing them into the ground in Florida as they do now. It was a sport designed for gracious living—the Sport of Kings, they called it. And during these years the Kentucky Derby emerged as the big single event the sport needed in order to gain identity with people across the country. In 1915, Cornelius Vanderbilt Whitney, Sr., shipped the filly, Regret, to Louisville and with Joe Notter riding, she took

179

the race. Regret was the first Eastern horse to be shipped to the Derby and she was also the only filly ever to win the Derby. In the spring, girl horses usually are more interested in being caught by boy horses then in outrunning them over a mile and a quarter. Which should settle the question of horses being dumb. This natural combination of recognition by a powerful stable such as Whitney's, plus the natural story surrounding a filly winning the race, was all an ex-tailor named Matt J. Winn needed to put the Kentucky Derby into an American sports classic. Winn, who placed a Colonel in front of his name, was a bourbon-drinking, cigar-smoking, magnificent liar who was president of Churchill Downs. He spoke lovingly of the bluegrass and lore of the Kentucky horse-breeding belt, but was cute enough to make his speeches from a suite in the Waldorf-Astoria in New York City, where people who counted would be able to listen to his build-up.

Everyplace else, this Golden Age of racing was for the rich, unhurried, and unworried, who did things in the grand style. However, despite its trappings of graciousness, these years also were wide open for anybody who wanted to take a shot at a private retirement fund. On Mr. Fitz's side of the track, it was still a place and always would be a place where horses had sesamoid trouble or split pasterns and anybody working on them properly didn't have time for anything else. But on the other side of the track, where the people are, a man who could think a little and had some daring to him could take it in big.

Bookmaker Johnny Walters was one. He had started his life selling programs at Sheepshead Bay. With a mind made for numbers, he became the biggest bet-taker of his time. When he opened shop each day, it was not for the purpose of grinding out a living. He had his eye on big money and would take a chance for it on any given day. It paid off. When he died they needed a couple of key rings to cover the packed safe deposit boxes he owned.

There was, for example, the afternoon at Aqueduct when

George H. Bull, the millionaire owner, came up to Walters in the clubhouse and bet $25 on his horse, Mustard Seed. The $25 was Bull's limit. A few minutes later, Bull came back, took the cigar out of his mouth and said he wanted to get down for $200 on the horse.

"Jack Goldsboro must like the horse," Walters said. Goldsboro, a crack horseman, trained for Bull. Walters would go along with this kind of an opinion.

"Mustard Seed right now can beat anything alive," Bull said. Walters nodded. He had the horse at 6–1 on his slate.

There was action coming on this race, Walters knew, because two of the heaviest gamblers of all time, Harry F. Sinclair and Payne Whitney, had horses entered in the race. Both customers, they would go heavy. And Walters was ready to go against them with Goldsboro's opinion.

Sinclair made his move in a few minutes. He put $35,000 down on his horse, Timeless. Payne Whitney followed with a $25,000 bet on his Sir George. Then Walters took in a pair of $10,000 bets on a horse called Replogel. The normal action on the race took place, too. As he grabbed the action, Walters' eyes narrowed and he started to figure. Normally, a bookmaking operation is a mathematical affair. There are the prices you lay on the horses. You can only take so much action on any one horse. If you are overloaded on a certain horse you must even it off. The normal thing to do is get rid of some of the overload—bet it off with another bookmaker. It is a game of percentages and quick thinking and if you don't know what you are doing you are a cinch to have your finances maimed or killed off altogether. But on this afternoon, Walters was taking the big shot. He gave orders to get off every dollar taken in on Mustard Seed. He was going to hold the rest. If Whitney's horse won he could have lost up to $200,000. If Sinclair's came in, he was going to be hit for $150,000. If Replogel came down on top, he would be out $200,000.

But taking chances was Walters' business. He stood like a statue and watched the race. When Mustard Seed started to draw clear in the last sixteenth Walters didn't even smile. He watched the horse go under the winner, then turned around and started talking with his assistants about the prices for the next race. He had just pocketed $80,000 for himself. But that was the last race. He was looking for the next one now.

These were years when a big bettor could operate. Under today's pari-mutuel system, it is insanity to do any heavy betting. The 16 per cent tax on all bets is too much percentage for anybody to give away and there is no chance to get an acceptable price because the mutuel machines have made Communism out of payoff prices. When a horse wins, everybody gets the same payoff. In this pre-mutuel era we're dealing with now, each bookmaker made his own prices and a man could shop. And if the price on a horse opened at 20–1 and you bet on it, then it subsequently was bet down to 6–1, you still had 20–1 going. But with the mutuels you can bet on it at any time, it doesn't matter. Bet early. Or bet at the last second. The payoff will be made on the post-time prices only. A big bettor in those times also did not have to face a game where the state and track jumped in and took that 16 per cent.

They were times where you could bet horses big. And there were men whose names never appear in the record books, but who bet enough to break Russia. One of them was a man named Colonel Samuel James who started out in life as a cotton planter in Louisiana, but in leisure time spent around the Fairgrounds track in New Orleans he came up with an idea which, as far as he was concerned, was six lengths better than the cotton gin. The Colonel, a tall, quiet man who wore a mustache, thought that a thing called time was the only way to rate race horses.

Most people who bet horses and ran them at this time were of the opinion that comparison was the only way to rate a horse. The class of a horse was determined by whom the horse had beaten and by what distance he had won by. But Colonel James felt time was all that counted. He brought this idea into New York, along with a thick book filled with timetables which had been developed by a Dr. Airth in London. The Colonel then went to work. He refused to accept the official time of a race as given by the track. He clocked races himself, breaking the fractions down to a hundredth of a second instead of the usual fifth of a second used by the tracks.

As there were no official cameras on the grounds, Colonel James took photos of all finishes himself. When developed, these showed margins and placings of also-rans which were not properly recorded in the newspaper charts. The Colonel began to knock the game apart with his theories.

Just as James was getting his system to work, a civil engineer named Robert Mensel was working on a road-building project in New Orleans. He was an industrious, homeloving non-drinker or gambler. Then he went to the track on an afternoon off from the job. It was a windy day and as he watched the first races of his life he began to wonder what the wind velocity meant to horses. Presently, he became quite occupied with this theory and a few winners with it changed his opinion of road-building and now he could be found at the New York tracks, placing an anemometer in the infield in order to get a wind reading. This was quickly applied to the intricate timing charts of Colonel James. Now under the wind theory, a head wind can do more to hinder a horse than a tail wind of the same velocity can help. It all sounds like gibberish and the horses still had to run around the track, but Colonel James and Mensel and Claude Kyle and Will Collins and others who went with these speed charts, as they are called, were out there banging away, day after day, and nobody ever had to go to work for a living.

"Value," Colonel James always said. "You must get value on your bets. To beat the races you must shop. You can, under ideal circumstances, win one third of your bets. Therefore, you must get 4–1 or better on an average bet in order to show a profit. If you were to take only 3–1, it would leave you even. In short races, where there is more chance for interference, you must get a bit better than 4–1. There must be value at all times. You must get even money on the 1–2 shot, or 5–1 on the horse that should be 8–5. Otherwise, there is no chance of profit.

It was a business on which James and the ones like him worked 12 to 14 hours a day, and worked with MIT precision. The 16 per cent takeout faced by today's players would have left James playing second cornet in a Salvation Army band. But in these days, with his time and wind and figures and value, he made out.

These were strange men, as are most professional gamblers. The common idea of a big gambler is a man who treats money as if it were confetti, can be found ringside at a night club if he's a winner and generally turns every day into a Saturday night in Sodom and Gomorrah. Which is exactly the way it is not. Colonel James, for example, made sure to buy straw hats when they were on sale in October in order to save a half dollar or so. Collins walked about with a great motto about the use of his money—"Go to Wall Street only on Sundays, holidays and days of panic." Otherwise, he wouldn't invest a dollar in the White House. But when panic hit the Street, Collins was there and he once got a little thing called Eastman-Kodak when it was rock bottom and when he died they needed three surrogates to cut up the money.

It was at this time, and over on the other side of the track from Mr. Fitz, that probably the best-known race-track betting maneuver of all time took place. It was at Aqueduct, on July 4, 1921, a 94-degree day that was thick with humidity. At 2:30 P.M. a man named Arnold Rothstein walked over to speak to Max Hirsch, his trainer. Max was heading for the race secretary's office.

"I'm scratching the horse, that all right with you?" Hirsch said.

"What's the matter with him?" Rothstein said.

"Nothing. You know the shape he's in. Perfect. But I'm thinking of dropping him in an overnight later in the week. Although any spot is a good one for him right now."

"Why scratch him then?" Rothstein said. "I'm always ready to win a bet."

"He's still in the barn at Belmont," Hirsch said.

"Get him here and get him running," Rothstein said.

Then Rothstein turned and headed for the clubhouse. He was going to start making bets on the horse, Sidereal, which was entered in the third race. Not just normal bets. But enough bets to satisfy an idea that had grown into an obsession with him. He wanted to win a million dollars on one horse race. And for some reason he just had made a snap judgment and picked this boiling afternoon to satisfy his urge. The horse he was going to try and win his million with was a two-year-old which had not won in the only three starts of his career. Bookmakers had Sidereal listed at 30–1.

It was, eighty-year-old Max Hirsch says today, a strange thing from the start. Rothstein had no plan. One minute it was just going to be a hot, humid day at the races. Then men forgot the heat because the biggest betting splurge of all time was taking place. It was typical of Rothstein.

Rothstein went into the clubhouse at Aqueduct on this day and started to dispatch his betting commissioners to get down on Sidereal for him. While Rothstein was doing this, Max Hirsch was on the telephone. There was a rule in racing that a horse must be in the paddock 30 minutes before post time or be automatically scratched from the race. It didn't leave Hirsch much time at all to get the horse from its barn at Belmont Park, six miles away from Aqueduct.

Max is a man who had been through all the thrills and disappointments and tense moments of racing, but this one was murder. With Rothstein's men out sending in money in alarming amounts—a guy named Morris the Boob leading them—Hirsch couldn't get anybody from his stable at Belmont Park to answer the phone. He kept hanging up and then calling again and then hanging up again and trying it once more. There was no dial system and the telephone company offices had no air conditioning. The operators, sluggish in the 94-

185

degree heat and high humidity, were slow about putting calls through. Hirsch was starting to get the shakes. Then he thought of his wife, who was at home, near Belmont. He got her on the phone, told her to get over to the stable and get the foreman to load Sidereal on the van and hustle him to Aqueduct.

Above Hirsch, in the stands, there was panic. Bookmakers kept scrubbing out the numbers next to Sidereal and putting smaller ones and finally when the price hit 5–1 and the late rush of Rothstein betting commissioners was on, most of them took the horse off the slate. It was getting too big for them.

Rothstein and his wife were sitting quietly in a box seat. He talked of the heat, a show on Broadway, a man he knew. His face showed nothing.

After the second race, the horses for the third were brought over from the stable area for saddling. Sidereal was missing. He was not on the grounds yet.

"Where's your horse?" Jimmy McLaughlin, paddock judge, asked Hirsch.

"He'll be right here," Max said. He had no idea whether his wife had gotten to the barn. But he did have a good idea of what the trip would be like for a horse van coming from Belmont Park on a holiday such as this. Two drunks driving from a swim at Valley Stream State Park could get in front of his van, start dawdling, and it would be good-by betting coup. And by now Hirsch knew all about the betting. He hadn't spoken to AR for a couple of hours, but all he had to do was listen to the moaning and questioning going on among bookmakers and he knew a big smash-up was being put together by his boss.

Hirsch stood nervously by the saddling stall assigned to Sidereal. All he could do was wait. Jockey Billy Kelsay, in Rothstein silks, stood beside him.

"Give you another minute, Max," McLaughlin said. "Then we'll have to scratch him."

The minute went by. Then there was a wave from the

other side of the track and here came Sidereal, led by a groom. Kelsay was swung up on the horse, wheeled him into the post parade and Hirsch walked over to the rail and leaned against it. He was shot. And it was out of his hands now. Upstairs, Rothstein put his field glasses on Sidereal and watched the horse as he went to the post. Sidereal had a fine head, it was stuck up there proudly. The sun broke on his curried coat and glared back at Rothstein's field glasses. The horse was in top condition.

The gambler never changed expression. The big ones never do. He stood there with his glasses on the race, his lips together, his hands without a quiver as the 13-horse field broke from the barrier in the five-eighths of a mile race. Ultimo, owned by Charles Stoneham, who also owned the New York Giants, took the lead. Northcliffe, second. Harry Payne Whitney's Brainstorm third. It went that way around the turn and into the stretch. Then Sidereal moved on the leaders. At the eight pole Sidereal hooked onto Ultimo. They came down together in one of those things where the horses keep nodding their heads up and down and the one who has his head up at the finish will win. If you have two dollars on one of these kind of races it does something to you. Not Rothstein. The binoculars never wavered. The lips stayed closed. Then with 20 yards to go, Sidereal got his head out. Then he gained with each lunge and went under the winner by a half-length. The time for the race was 59 2/5. The winner's purse was $1172.94.

Rothstein took his glasses down and sat down. Morris the Boob and his other betting commissioners came to him, whispered, then walked away. Rothstein nodded his head. It was all right, this one. But not right enough. He had won $850,000. It still wasn't a million.

It was this kind of an era. And in the middle of it, Mr. Fitz came within a wave of the hand or two of getting his hands on what still is considered the greatest horse ever to step onto a race track. He saw the horse the first time on a hot August morning in 1918 at Saratoga. August Belmont was selling his yearlings, and now, two days before the auction, Mr. Fitz was walking along the shedrow of Belmont's yearling barn, looking over the stock carefully. They were all well-bred, good-looking animals, but one of them caught Mr. Fitz's eye. The colt was a chestnut and he was going to grow into an outsized animal, too. The tag posted on the green-painted wood alongside the stall said the horse was by Fair Play out of Mahubah.

That night, he called Johnson in New York and told him about the horse.

"If you're going to come up and buy anything, that's the one I'd take," he told Johnson.

But the day of the auction, Johnson was stuck on business down in New York and he told Mr. Fitz to go out and do the bidding. Which helped bring about the crime of the century. For if Johnson were on the scene and his trainer liked the horse, he would have gone for the works and gotten the horse with little trouble.

Mr. Fitz, however, had total caution when it came to spending somebody else's money and when a groom wearing a white dinner jacket led Belmont's big yearling into the sales ring at the auction, Johnson's money was in safe hands. Too safe.

The auctioneer announced the horse's background, then started the bidding at $2500.

Mr. Fitz waved his program and the auctioneer caught that and it put him in the bidding. A man named Samuel D. Riddle got in, too. There were many others, but they dropped out and there were only a couple left as the price went up to $4000, then $4200 and $4400 and finally, at $4600, Mr. Fitz stopped.

"If it were my money it'd be a different thing," he said when he got out of the bidding. "But I don't like throwin' Mr. Johnson's money around with him not here. That ain't my kind of a game. I know one thing. If Johnson was here and he knew I liked the horse this much he'd start biddin' and get him in a second."

Riddle was getting a little touchy about it right about here, too, and before they got him to $5000 and knocked down the horse to him, Riddle did considerable seat-writhing. When he got the horse, Riddle went home and started writing out names. He came up with one he thought was good. The Jockey Club allowed him to register it. The name was Man o' War and there are old men around today whose eyes water when they tell you of this horse. Big Red, they called him, and he started 21 times in his life and was beaten only once and he became a part of American lore. His groom, Will Harbut, retired to Kentucky with the horse and spent his time proudly bringing out Big Red for visitors and telling them, "Dis de mostest horse ever."

One year later, and again at Saratoga, Mr. Fitz took another loss with the big horse. For some reason which he can't account for now, and probably has bawled himself out for over the years, he was standing around before one of Man o' War's races, took a look at the price, 1–2, and decided to get a little easy money. He bet a hundred on Man o' War. It was a day that was to become famous in racing history for other reasons than Fitzsimmons betting $100. Man o' War's regular rider, Clarence Kummer, came up sick at the last minute and jockey Johnny Loftus was put on to replace him. Actually, Loftus did not feel too well himself. Anyhow, when they left the post, Willie Knapp, on a horse called Upset, had a big lead. Too big. Man o' War came on with a tremendous rush at the end, but he had too much to make up. He was second for the only time in his life.

"I could have just as easy bought the horse and he could have turned out to be nothin' much at all," Mr. Fitz figures. "He was just a nice-lookin' kind of a colt. Never worried me that I didn't get him. But the bet, that's a different thing. I must of lost my brains. Hasn't been a horse yet worth a hundred-dollar bet."

The little Man o' War item put aside, Mr. Fitz was a natural in the business of buying race horses. Now at times, and particularly at all times, this can be a hazardous business.

There is something that happens to a Kentucky breeder when he stands next to a horse of his and talks to somebody who wants to buy the horse. The barn can be quiet and the sloping, fenced-in fields around it can be a beautiful sight. But when a breeder is selling a horse you can hear him saying to himself the principles of his trade, as set down by David Harum: "Do unto the other fella as he would do unto you —only do it furst."

You get a belly full of fried chicken when you go to a horse farm with money in your pocket. You get bourbon. All the bourbon the man can get you to take. After that, you're on your own. The horse is alive. You can be sure of that. They'll put a mirror in front of his nostrils to prove he can breathe. After this, just duck.

Mr. Fitz never had any trouble with this part of it at all. He and Johnson made a couple of trips to Lexington and didn't come close to making a bad move. In 1919, Mr. Fitz prowled breeder Arthur B. Hancock's Clairborne Farm for a couple of days, watching the yearlings closely. He picked out twenty-two. Johnson purchased them for a package price of $40,000. The horses were shipped up to Mr. Fitz at Gravesend and within a year, Max Hirsch, dealing for Rothstein, had bought seven of them for $72,000 and still in the barn was a horse called Knobbie and another called Playfellow, who was a full brother to Man o' War. Knobbie later was sold to Trainer Sam Hildreth of the Rancocas Stable, owned by Harry F. Sinclair, for $60,000. In 1921, Hildreth came around again. He wanted to look at Playfellow.

Playfellow, a huge animal, had been a bust as a two-year-old and looked to be nothing at three. But he suddenly broke out with two races at Aqueduct that had everybody talking about him. The horse, they said, was just a big, strapping thing that had needed time. Now he was ready to run like a great one, they said. The hysteria over Man o' War made Play-fellow, Big Red's full brother, a headline animal.

Sinclair wanted Playfellow. He had Hildreth make several visits to Mr. Fitz's barn to look over the horse. Then he offered Johnson $115,000 for the horse. Mr. Fitz thought the horse was going to be a big winner, but it was too much money for Johnson to turn down. He took the offer. He was now playing in big money with Harry F. Sinclair, a man who was to rock the country with maneuverings that history books call the Teapot Dome scandals. People usually didn't do well playing with Sinclair. Johnson found that out. He left racing because of it.

Playfellow was a huge horse who ate as much as you would give him and needed a lot of work to stay in shape. Hildreth was a trainer who was not known for working horses too strenuously. So Playfellow settled down in the great Rancocas barn and loaded up on more food than anybody had ever seen and Hildreth worked him lightly. When Hildreth put the horse in a race, Playfellow ran like a bartender. He was third in his first start. A bad third. So bad that people were laughing at Sinclair. The papers put it in headlines; the sharpsters, Sinclair and Hildreth, had bought a $115,000 lemon.

Sinclair sat down that night and began to think. He wanted an angle. When Sinclair started to think of angles he usually was good. This time, as Mr. Fitz found out, he was very good.

"Fitzsimmons and Johnson sold us a horse that is a wind sucker and a cribber," Sinclair announced the next morning. "We are going to court to get the money back."

A wind sucker is a horse that makes a funnel of his tongue and draws great rushes of air into his stomach. This is supposed to load him up with so much air that he cannot run properly. A cribber is along the same lines. He sinks his teeth into a piece of wood, a railing or the feed box, and then sucks in air. Both these habits are not good and many times can't be corrected.

Mr. Fitz thought it was a joke. There had been nothing

wrong with Playfellow when the horse put together his two
big races for him.

"It was an honest sale, and he was a good horse when he left
this barn," Mr. Fitz said. "Hildreth should've worked him a
little harder, that's all."

This was enough for the people who knew Mr. Fitz. But
they were people on a race track. They were not people in a
courtroom, which is a place where money has accomplished
many things. In March of 1922, the suit of Harry F. Sinclair
vs. James Johnson was opened in Brooklyn Supreme Court.
It was a joke. First, Mr. Fitz's night watchman, George Travers,
took the stand. He was a man who couldn't hear a fire bell if
you put it next to his ear, but on the stand he was by Sono-
tone out of Zenith. Yes, he said, he knew the horse was a wind
sucker. He heard the horse sucking wind every night in Mr.
Fitz's barn.

Then Snapper Garrison appeared. Mr. Fitz wondered what
he could know about Playfellow. It turned out Snapper knew
a lot. Why, he testified, he had been in Mr. Fitz's barn at ten
o'clock one morning and he had seen Playfellow cribbing on
a feedbox in the stall. He also claimed that nobody was on
the premises—something that hasn't been true of a Fitzsimmons operation in seventy-six years.

The jury took the case, stayed behind closed doors throughout the afternoon, and then returned with a verdict in favor
of Sinclair. Johnson had to give back the money. Later he
tried an appeal, but got nowhere.

The Playfellow suit disheartened Johnson. He started to sell
off his horses and get out of racing. He didn't like games where
rich men could cheat and get away with it. Mr. Fitz had no
trouble picking up more horses to train. More important to
him, he had no anger in him at all over the lawsuit.

"Hildreth? He's a fine fella," Mr. Fitz said. "Garrison? Oh,
Snapper, I like him. We always had good times together. The
watchman? He was a real good night watchman."

11 Dark Secret at the finish of the Jockey Club Gold Cup Race at Belmont

12 Mr. Fitz and Eddie Arcaro (1961)

13 The famous distance
horse Diavolo trained by
Mr. Fitz winning the
Tremont Stakes at
Aqueduct (1927)

14 Mr. Fitz and Johnny
Longden (1961)
(*Mike Sirico*)

15 A photograph of a painting of Sunny Jim done from life at Saratoga in 1960 by Robert Roché. Courtesy of the New York Racing Association.

16 Mr. Fitz watching the post parade at Aqueduct (1960) *(New York Times)*

17 Mr. Fitz watching the races at Hialeah *(Wide World Photos)*

18 Mr. Fitz in the doorway of his Barn 17 at Belmont Race Track
(UPI photo by Joel Schrank)

"You see," this old man tells you, "you've got to think of the other fella. Give him the best of it all the time. Maybe there's reasons why people do things. Give them the edge. Then you'll never have to go around not liking anybody."

10. The Big Years

On a Saturday afternoon in November of 1923, Mr. Fitz was coming into the paddock at Pimlico race track just as a man named William Woodward was leaving. Woodward was a quiet, austere man who had a mustache, straight, matted-down hair and a checkbook in his inside coat pocket that no fountain pen would ever whack out. Woodward was connected with a little business establishment in New York known as the Hanover National Bank, and he owned a tremendous racing establishment known as Belair Stud Farm. Mr. Fitz never had met Woodward, except to nod hello around a race track, but this time Woodward came right up to him.

"Fitz, I'd like to speak to you," he said. "Would you like to train my horses?"

"Love it."

"Fine. Supposing you come out to my farm tomorrow and we'll talk about it."

The next day Mr. Fitz and Woodward spoke. They used few words. Did Mr. Fitz want a contract? No. He didn't believe in them things. Fine. Was there anything else? Oh, yes. Those few horses owned by Maxwell and Pratt. He wanted to keep them. Oh, that can be arranged. Anything else? Nothing.

Mr. Fitz left the rolling Belair Stud Farm that afternoon

with everything. After thirty-eight years, it all fell into place. You could take all the worry and heartache and patience it took to last and throw them out because now there were going to be only big days for Mr. Fitz. He had a ton of hard-gained ability. All of a sudden, in one afternoon, Mr. Fitz had the whole thing beat.

He went back to Pimlico to check on his horses, then went to a movie. Monday morning he was making arrangements at Aqueduct for additional barn space. He was going to have new horses moving in, he told the track officials. After thirty-eight years of trying to get there, he was a little out of the range of excitement.

From then on, he was a part of some of the biggest days in American racing history. A year later, a quiet, gentle woman named Mrs. Henry Carnegie Phipps and her brother, Ogden L. Mills, who would later become Secretary of the Treasury in President Hoover's Cabinet, came to him and asked if he could handle their Wheatley Stable. Woodward said it was fine. Mr. Fitz took their horses on, and between Belair and Wheatley he was to have as close to a corner on the racing market as you could get.

The first year with Belair, Mr. Fitz had a horse called the Aga Kahn who could run with anything on four feet. The Wheatley Stable's first big horse came a couple of years later. It was Dice. He won five starts as a two-year-old and looked like he could be just about anything you wanted to say about him. But one morning at Saratoga the horse broke a blood vessel while he was working out and when he got back to Mr. Fitz he was in distress. Nobody could figure out why. By the time the veterinarian found the trouble, the horse had bled to death internally. It was the worst kind of luck you can have, but it didn't get Mr. Fitz down.

Part of Mr. Fitz's arrangement with Belair called for him to check the farm during the spring and fall and look over the horses Woodward had bred and was raising down there. Young thoroughbred horses on a high-class breeding farm all seem to look equal if you are an outsider. And even the best horsemen can't see too much difference in them. With a race horse, just as a human being, you have to throw him into the game and let him go at it. You can never see things like courage simply by looking.

One afternoon in the spring of 1928, Mr. Fitz and Woodward hung over a fence at Belair and took a look at a group of yearlings which would be sorted out, the best of them to be broken for racing and put on the track under Mr. Fitz's care the next year. One of them was a blaze-faced colt sired by Sir Gallahad III, an imported stallion. Woodward was a man whose greatest delight came in the tedious, nebulous business of figuring out which stallion and which dam would produce the best offspring. He leaned heavily toward Sir Gallahad III as a sire, so he was more than ordinarily interested in the colt. He regarded the colt as a possible proof that his notions on how to tinker with the family tree of a horse were correct.

Mr. Fitz wasn't that lofty. He was more interested in the horse's nostrils.

"They're a little small for my tastes," he was saying. "They have trouble breathin' during a race if the nostrils ain't big enough. I wish his were a little wider. Horse don't seem to have much to breathe with up there. We'll just have to take 'em and see what he can do."

Woodward said something about naming the horse Gallant Fox. Then they went on to look at the next.

The next year, Gallant Fox was in the Fitzsimmons barn at Aqueduct, about as lazy an animal as anybody ever came across. He would run with another horse in the morning, then stop dead the minute he passed him. Mr. Fitz put a second horse halfway around and when Gallant Fox got there he found he had another horse to beat and that finally kept him going. But if you didn't play tricks with him he'd do everything but lean against the rail and fall asleep. In his first couple of starts, Gallant Fox was well out of it. But Mr. Fitz saw one thing in him: the horse was coming on at the end every time.

Since early two-year-old races are for short distances, it looked like he simply needed more ground to cover. He got it at Saratoga, winning two races, the Flash and Junior Champion Stakes, and he looked like a lock for the rich Futurity that fall at Belmont Park. He seemed to be able to suck in enough air through those nostrils to give a car a run for it.

Mr. Fitz thought so, too. When the horses went to the gate for the Futurity, he walked into the infield and stood near the wire of the Widener Chute, a straight course which bisected the running oval and was used for major two-year-old races. He had spent a lot of time trying to get a little more pep into Gallant Fox during the early part of a race, so now, as he watched the flashes of silk in the starting gate, he was looking for the red polka dots of Belair. He wanted to see his work pay dividends. The Fox would come out running a little better this time, he thought. This wouldn't hurt anybody, either. The Futurity is big at the bank. Then the bell rang, the flaps banged open and here came Whichone going to the lead, with a horse called Hi-jack right on him. Somewhere back in the dust-clouded, bobbing mass of horses was Gallant Fox. He had thrown a no-'count start at Mr. Fitz, and now Gallant Fox had to come on like hell at the end to get third money. Whichone took first, which carried the slight matter of $76,520 to it. If Mr. Fitz's charge had won the race, he would have been counting out almost eight grand for the bank teller on Monday. Instead, he had nothing to do but go back to work and try to get Gallant Fox to run a little better a lot earlier. He turned around and started walking toward the gap in the infield rail. Nobody said much to Mr. Fitz. It's better not to talk to a man who loses a tough one like this. John Fitzsimmons walked up to meet his father at the gap. Even he was ready to be extra quiet. Mr. Fitz came up to him, didn't even break stride, and John fell in beside him.

"Say, Johnny," Mr. Fitz said, "what's playin' at the movie down in Sheepshead Bay tonight?"

He never mentioned the race again.

By the next spring, there was no rap you could put on Gallant Fox. He filled out over the winter and now his muscles bulged inside his sleek coat and he looked like he could run through a brick wall. He was now the first of the great horses for Mr. Fitz, the one who could get it all. He looked every inch of that. So much so that one afternoon, for the first time, Woodward came out to the barn to talk to him about the handling of a horse. From the day they shook hands on the farm in Maryland, Woodward and Mr. Fitz had the kind of relationship anybody trying to do a good job should have. Woodward had hired a trainer, and under no circumstances would he interfere with his man. "How are you?" is the only question Woodward ever asked. This time, however, he wanted to have a say. The horse was the first Woodward ever fell in love with, and people are a little different when this happens.

"Fitz," he said, "wouldn't it be good if we got a regular rider for this horse?"

"Yes, it would," Mr. Fitz agreed. "Who would you like to get?"

"Who would you like?"

"The fella that can do the best job."

The fella who could do the best job, they agreed, was Earl Sande. The year before, Sande had gone down in a terrible fall. When he got out of the hospital he had decided to retire from riding. He had won Kentucky Derbies on Zev and Flying Ebony. He had ridden Man o' War and Grey Lag and Mad Play and Chance Shot. He had money, wanted to be a trainer and own the horses himself. He felt he was through taking risks. The fall made him decide to get out. But after laying around for a full year—he was up on only ten horses in 1929, with only one winner—Sande found that money, if you kept sending it out and not replacing it, could become something of a problem. He decided to come back to riding horses. Everybody waited to see what kind of shape he was in, but Mr. Fitz and Woodward didn't bother. Mr. Fitz knew enough about Sande. Earl had gristle inside his stomach and a heart that pumped the bright and rich red blood that runs in only the few. Sande had the confidence that goes with it, too. When Woodward offered him a flat fee of $10,000 to ride Gallant Fox for the year, Earl turned it down. He had seen enough of Gallant Fox to know what he had. He wanted 10 per cent of all the purses he won.

"We're going to win a lot of races," he said. He got his percentage deal.

Mr. Fitz began to put Gallant Fox in shape for the big three-year-old races. First there were the long gallops, overly long, it seemed to most horse people on the grounds. Then he began to set him down in a series of speed works that seemed to be brutal. It is Mr. Fitz's way to train a horse. This big, royally bred animal could take all you threw at him, he figured. He never has babied a horse.

"You got to get them to do what they're raised for," he insists. "Spoil 'em and you're ruining their chances."

On Saturday, April 26, 1930, Gallant Fox was standing in the saddling enclosure at Jamaica race track with Fish Tappen and a groom around him while Mr. Fitz and Sande stood and talked quietly about what to do in the Wood Memorial, which was to be run in a couple of minutes. Woodward was off to one side. He had put his hand into the business with Gallant Fox just once. He would never say another thing for the rest of his life. Then Sande got up on Gallant Fox, went out on the track and won by five lengths, running away from a horse called Crack Brigade and another called Desert Light. It was no contest at all and after it, in the clubhouse, Tom Shaw, the bookmaker, turned around and began quoting a new price on Gallant Fox in the Kentucky Derby. Gallant Fox had been 8–1. He now was 4–1.

The Preakness at Pimlico was to come first. It was run a week before the Derby at this time. So on May 9, coming around the tight last turn at Pimlico, Crack Brigade was showing the way. But Gallant Fox moved to him as the track became straight. They started down the stretch as one. At the sixteenth pole, Gallant Fox got his head in front, then began to draw away. The official margin was three parts of a length and after the race Mr. Fitz was arranging for transportation to Louisville and the Derby for Gallant Fox. Then he went back to Aqueduct where, on Monday morning, he'd be up taking care of the rest of the horses.

Fish Tappen went to Churchill Downs with Gallant Fox. He had the horse out on the track for a light workout Monday. Mr. Fitz was at Aqueduct. Tappen took care of the horse on Tuesday, too. Mr. Fitz stayed in New York with the rest of the horses. On Wednesday, Tappen gave the Fox his big prep for the race. He brought the horse through the gap from the barn area and onto the track early, while a mob followed after him, looking and taking notes and asking questions. At Churchill Downs, the Derby favorite always gets an entourage which looks in awe at the horse, and follows him constantly. The horse returns this affection by trying to sink his teeth into the shoulder of the nearest idiot. Tappen, never given to speeches, stationed himself against the rail while Sande, singing softly to Gallant Fox in the morning air, started off down the track. He galloped easily over to the head of the stretch, then took off. The work was for the full Derby distance of a mile and a quarter. This race always is the first time in a horse's life that he goes this far. The big question before it always centers on whether the horse can last the distance. Mr. Fitz's answer to this always has been "sure he can go a mile and a quarter. Question is, can he run it fast enough." On this particular morning there seemed to be legitimate concern over Gallant Fox's ability even to finish the workout. The horse wasn't interested in any workout on any race track on this day. Sande wasn't pressing him, either. So the horse took his time about things and negotiated the distance in 2:19.

Up in the grandstand, Tommy Oliphant, the clocker, punched his watch as Gallant Fox finished the work. He looked at it, then shook his head.

"He run it in trottin' horse time."

Mr. Fitz still was at Aqueduct supervising his stable. Fish called him in mid-morning, told him about the work, and both agreed it was fine.

"I'll be down tomorrow," Mr. Fitz said.

Around Louisville, they were trying to figure out what was going on. Here was the Derby favorite working like a milk horse and his trainer hadn't even bothered to come down and supervise the horse personally for a race that was, by now, the biggest in the country. It was something they were to wonder about whenever Mr. Fitz came up with a big horse. He has always conducted his business on the theory that a weak horse, just like a weak child, needs all the work. The big one is better off if left alone when he gets in form. Gallant Fox was in form. He was coming off a good race. But up at Aqueduct Mr. Fitz had fifty-one other horses, some of them nervous animals that needed a lot of work before they'd come around and run properly. He left Gallant Fox alone.

"Gallant Fox?" Mr. Fitz was saying, "what am I going to do with him, except run him Saturday? I'd be wastin' my time down there."

So on Thursday, jacket slung over his arm, suspenders bunching up his shirt, an outrageous tie setting it all off, James E. Fitzsimmons came into Louisville by train for the most glamorous race in the country. He had Gallant Fox on the track Friday morning for a three-furlong tightener, then sent the horse back to the barn and he and Fish went to the movies.

On Saturday, the cramped saddling enclosures at Churchill Downs was crowded with owners, trainers, and officials, and by the time Earl Sande and the rest of the riders came down the wooden stairs from the jockeys' room, the tension had reached its peak. Then the jocks got up, the outriders started to lead the field out to the track and one of racing's great moments was about to take place. Mr. Fitz and Tappen trailed along. They were through playing "My Old Kentucky Home" by the time Mr. Fitz came out of the tunnel, and there wasn't a place you could find to sit or stand and still see the race. Fish and Mr. Fitz walked across the track to the winner's circle, which was empty. It seemed like a good spot. But as the horses started to jog toward the starting gate, a couple of uniformed track police hustled toward them.

"We got to clear this place out," they told Mr. Fitz. "You all have to go over there. You watch the race from there. We can't have you standin' here."

Mr. Fitz did not say who he was. He didn't think that would matter. So he let the cops steer him into the packed infield. The people all were crammed against a wire fence, in good position to shove and push and crane their necks and see, at best, almost nothing of the race. Mr. Fitz was wedged between onlookers when the track announcer said it was post time. He was still jammed there when the crowd gave a big roar. Here they come, somebody yelled. Here was the biggest moment in Mr. Fitz's life and he was looking squarely at the neck of some guy from Evansville who needed a haircut.

The crowd was roaring for some time before he got a glimpse of the race. Alcibiades on the lead, with Buckey Poet pressing and Tannery trying to run with them. Running fifth, free of trouble, was Gallant Fox. The field headed down the track toward the first turn and that was the last Mr. Fitz saw of them for a long time. When he picked up the horses again, they were way over on the other side of the track. But this time he didn't mind the mess at all. Because Sande had Gallant Fox going now. He had moved on the first flight of horses going around the turn and now down the backstretch he brought Gallant Fox up to Alcibiades, then ran along with him for awhile. Gallant Fox loved it. He began to reach out and dig in. He taunted the other horse. Come on and run, he was saying. Alcibiades tried to stay with him, but Gallant Fox knocked him out and pulled away by two lengths. Then Mr. Fitz couldn't see the horses again. The crowd was in the way. But the track announcer kept saying it was Gallant Fox on the lead. And Sande was holding him there. Earl had ridden perfectly so far. He had kept his horse out of trouble every foot of the way. He hadn't done a thing to use up any more of Gallant Fox than necessary. Now he came around the last turn with a ton of live horse under him and the big crowd began to roar as the great rider of his time hunched low on Gallant Fox's back, his body moving as if he were part of the horse, and the two of them came down the stretch with the rhythm of the big winner. With a sixteenth of a mile left to go, Mr. Fitz finally saw his horse again and it was something. Gallant Fox looked like a Currier & Ives print. He was moving along majestically, two lengths to the good; it could have been five or six any time he wanted. His blazed face and red-hooded head was nodding playfully. Mr. Fitz could see it all. The guy who needed a haircut had moved his head to one side for awhile.

High up in the press box atop the Churchill Downs roof, a thin man, glasses perched on his nose, teeth clamped on a pencil, began to hit the shift key on his typewriter in a nervous moment. Then he began to type. When he finished the first page he gave it to a telegrapher who started to tap it out in Morse code. It read:

dpr collect, sports, new york american

derby lead . . .

By Damon Runyon

LOUISVILLE, May 19—Say, have they turned back the ages,
Back to a Derby out of the yore?
Say, don't tell me I'm daffy,
Ain't that the same old grin?
Why it's that Handy Guy Named Sande
Bootin' them Babies in.

It was one of the greatest newspaper stories ever written about sports. It was all for Sande, who was in the winner's circle now on his third Kentucky Derby winner. They were putting a big blanket of roses over Gallant Fox's neck and the crowd back in the stands was cheering for the jockey. Sande had made a big comeback. He ranked alongside Babe Ruth, Bobby Jones, Red Grange, Bill Tilden, Walter Hagen, and Jack Dempsey in what they always call the Golden Age of Sports. It was a tremendous day for him.

Mr. Fitz didn't know a thing about all of this. He and Fish were trying to get out of the infield and get over to the barn so they could get a look at Gallant Fox. A half hour later, while Colonel Matt J. Winn, the Churchill Downs president, was pouring champagne for Woodward, Sande, and other dignitaries, Mr. Fitz was over on the other side of the track, leaning against the shedrow while a groom hot-walked Gallant Fox.

"He's fine, boss," the groom was saying. "He's a great one, ain't he?"

"Never mind the talk," Mr. Fitz said. "Give him a little bit of water, then keep him walkin'. This ain't a popularity contest."

"What are we goin' to do for celebratin'? We going to have a party?"

"We'll have a party. Monday morning at Aqueduct we'll have a party. It'll start at five in the morning."

Mr. Fitz was hitting it sky-high now, but as far as Jennie Fitzsimmons was concerned, none of it really mattered. She never had cared when the man used to come home at night with a dollar and maybe some loose change in his pocket. Now that he was coming home with checks for $10,000 in his wallet, she was most certainly not about to change. The money meant nothing. Anything that it brought meant less. She took whatever she was handed and promptly gave it away. There is no way to tell what Jennie gave away during her lifetime, but since this was her main pleasure in life it is taken for granted that she gave away an awful lot. Here and there, over the years, her family has, in fact, seen signs of it.

One Sunday morning some few years ago, Jack Fitzsimmons, a grandson, was at Mass in the Immaculate Heart of Mary Roman Catholic Church in San Antonio, Texas, which was near the Army post where he was stationed. On the way out, he happened to look at the thick pillars, all of which carried a brass plaque with the name of the person who donated the money to build the pillar. One of them read, DONATED BY JENNIE HARVEY FITZSIMMONS OF SHEEPSHEAD BAY, NEW YORK.

Her whole life was this way. It consisted of a series of days in which she tried to do something for somebody. Anybody. It didn't matter who. Even if it happened to be a dog. Mrs. Fitzsimmons at one time had a dog named Jerry, who had some collie in him and an appetite usually found in bears. He turned up missing one day and remained that way through several newspaper ads. Finally, he was found in another part of Brooklyn, a good half-hour away. With nobody around at the moment to drive over and collect the dog, Mrs. Fitzsimmons called for a taxi. She gave the driver the address and asked him to pick up the party and bring him back.

When the hackie found what the party was he exploded. When the party tried to lick the back of his neck on the drive home, the hackie was certain the dog was trying to take his head off. The trip became a series of near accidents.

At red lights, the hackie also took abuse from anybody who happened to see Jerry sitting proudly on the back seat, the way he always did in a car, and the meter clocking away. The meter ran almost eight dollars for the trip, a good job if you drive cabs, but when the hackie finished his run and deposited the dog, he made a solemn oath that the next call coming from the Fitzsimmons house would have to be for a human being.

The dog was an important thing in her life, as any of the Fitzsimmons offspring who rode in cars were to find out. Each August, Nana, as they called Jennie Fitzsimmons, would get into a car containing John, his wife Mae, seven or eight children and Jerry and start off for the month at Saratoga. The

dog would start the trip on the floor, which was not his style
at all. He was not backward about letting it be known, either.
After a half hour of Jerry's shifting around and dog-moaning,
Nana would tap one of the children and say, "Now you be
good and stand up for a while and let Jerry sit." The one
tapped would get up and Jerry would take a seat and ride
the rest of the way to Saratoga in style.

Wherever the Fitzsimmons family has gone since about
1925, it has been something of a migration. And until she died
in 1951, the people around her, and what she could do for
them, became Jennie Fitzsimmons' life. She had been through
too much to be excited about any success. A win in the Kentucky Derby? Oh, that would be fine. But if Mr. Fitz's horse
blew it, that would be all right, too. There was nothing to get
excited about. She had more important things at hand right in
Sheepshead Bay. Her son John was living in the house. He
had six children. Jimmy was across the street. He had three
children. Harvey was across the street, too. He had one child.
Next door were Mr. Fitz's sister, Aunt Nora, and his brother
Tom. And Edith and George and Harold and their children all
lived nearby. At night, Mr. Fitz's house was converted into a
restaurant. The kids would eat there, so would any of their
friends who happened to be around. Adults came in on the
second wave. On a good night you would have forty people
at dinner. On nights that were slow because of bad weather
or another attraction someplace—the usual things that mean
bad box office anywhere—only fifteen or thereabouts would
be on hand. Granddaughter Kathleen, as she got a little older,
began to make a rather big thing of Sunday breakfasts after
church. She could guarantee a turnout of twenty without even
starting to draw on the closest kin.

On a Saturday, when Mr. Fitz would be out at the track
running horses in the biggest races in America, his wife would
gather anywhere from fifteen to twenty children, take them
to the worst horror movie she could find in Brooklyn, and sit
directly behind them. When the kids froze during the scariest

part of the film, she'd have a field day. She would pinch one girl on the arm and get a scream out of her. Then she'd hit a boy on the head with a rolled-up newspaper and he'd jump a foot. The picture called *Dracula,* in which Bela Lugosi did everything but eat cameramen, was her all-time favorite.

She also made good use of a radio show called the "Witches' Tales." For this one, she would get the kids into her sitting room, demand that the lights be put out and then, in the dark, she'd shiver and moan and get the rest of them stiff with fear. Then she'd reach out, pinch the one who was frightened most, and start a riot.

For the Saratoga season, Mr. Fitz took a house on Lake Avenue that had six bedrooms, two dining rooms, a kitchen big enough to cook for an Automat, and a cottage in the back. The place was terribly inadequate. One dining room, used for the children, was just large enough to take care of them. The second one was fine for the adults, except you had to walk around a trunk placed against one wall. The trunk served, one year, as the support for John Fitzsimmons' bed for one three-week period in which there were too many people to fit into bedrooms. The menu for Sunday dinner became a rather constant affair—chicken. It took exactly thirty-six pounds of chicken to feed the mob.

Saratoga became so preposterous that Mrs. Fitzsimmons needed three women there to help her get through the season alive. Ella Lee, a domestic who was her only concession to success in Sheepshead Bay, came up. And Sarah and her cousin Min came from the track, lived in the cottage behind the house, and were around for the heavy times.

The size of the family gave Mr. Fitz's wife a lot of trouble when it came to her favorite pastime of giving things away. Every present she got, no matter what it was, was given to somebody else as quickly as possible. Most of the time, however, she could not remember who had given her the present originally. This usually got her into as many fixes as anybody could put together.

After one Christmas, she called in John and between hushes handed him a silver cocktail shaker and glasses.

"Don't say anything about this," she cautioned him. "I don't want to hurt anybody's feelings. If the person who gave me this knew I was giving it away they'd be badly hurt. Now you take this, I don't have any use for it. But whatever you do, keep it quiet."

John, who had given her the present himself, solemnly promised to be quiet.

She had a list of organizations and charities which apparently was sprawling. The family found that out when she died. At the wake one night, the Sheepshead Bay American Legion post, uniformed, flag-bearing, two-hundred strong, arrived at the house to conduct military services for the departed. She was, the commander explained, one of the post's stanchest financial backers. If Jennie Harvey Fitzsimmons had been alive at the moment she would have thrown a fit.

She gave away everything that wasn't nailed down. Mr. Fitz, in a burst of affluence, bought her an automatic dishwasher in the late '30s, an appliance found only at that time on Park Avenue or in a manor house. His wife thought it was great and she made much noise over it. Two days later, when everybody was out of the house, she was telling the moving men to be extra careful as they packed it onto a truck for delivery to the convent at St. Mark's Roman Catholic Church. She gave away her clothes, her husband's clothes—anything they had.

She read nearly everything printed, except stories on horses. She could argue the stock market, fashions or politics. World affairs in particular intrigued her. When President Truman recalled General MacArthur from Korea in 1951 she was beside herself. When she died suddenly the next day from the only heart attack of her life, everybody thought the headlines had something to do with it. But a story in the paper about her husband, of which there were several each week, was something to skip over. She knew too much about the subject to take anybody else's views on it. Besides, the stories always were about success, a topic which bored her.

She and Mr. Fitz were impossible moviegoers. On winter Saturdays in the years before Mr. Fitz had to race horses in Florida, he would have little to do, and the two would leave the house in the morning, catch a movie in Brooklyn, have lunch, see another one in New York, go to dinner someplace, then see a third at night. It was the closest thing to an entertainment splurge you could find them doing.

"She'd come to the track on Saturday, have a couple of the kids with her, but it would only be for lunch," Mr. Fitz says. "You could have the horses, as far as she was concerned. She'd go home when the races started. Every time she saw a track it reminded her of them two fellas that got killed and all the hard days we had to go through. And she didn't care for any of the talk when we were going good."

Besides, she had too many other things to do. For example, as part of her give-away program, Jennie Fitzsimmons was insistent that anybody in Sheepshead Bay, or practically anybody, who was without a home for one reason or another could find one at 1174 Sheepshead Bay Road. Her method for dealing with this problem of others was simple. Somebody in the family just had to move over.

11. For the Record

On the Monday after Gallant Fox won the 1930 Kentucky Derby, the sun was just starting to gleam on the short-cropped, wet grass of Aqueduct's infield when Mr. Fitz came to the rail, stop watch in hand, while Petee Wrack who was being pointed for the Suburban Handicap, bowed his neck against the exercise boy's hold, and started to thump down the track to begin his workout.

This is the way of the professional. Mr. Fitz had just won a Kentucky Derby, but here he was at work, first chance after it, just as he would have been if he had lost. The glamour and excitement and handshaking is for amateurs who have to be told that they are good. The big guy doesn't need it. He goes back to the job. You don't find much of this. For an obvious reason. Most people are amateurs.

Mr. Fitz shipped Gallant Fox to Belmont Park a few days later to get him ready for the Belmont Stakes, the last part of the Triple Crown. In the meantime he took the Suburban with Petee Wrack, a half-brother to Gallant Fox. And Whichone, Harry Payne Whitney's colt, came from way out of it with Sonny Workman up to win the Withers. Bookmakers promptly made him even money for the Belmont, June 7.

They were wasting their chalk. Even when Sande showed

up Friday morning with a couple of black eyes and patches over his face from an auto accident of the night before, it didn't change things. Sande got on the horse, worked him a half mile in 47 seconds, rode him out to five furlongs in one minute flat. When he got off, Mr. Fitz knew both horse and rider could take care of things.

Which they did the next day. Gallant Fox slammed out of the gate and seemed full of run on the rain-soaked track. Around him, Sande could see the wet dirt spraying into the air with each stride of the big field of horses. To hell with getting that dirt into my face, he said. It'll reopen all the cuts under my eyes. It was all he had to think about. He tapped Gallant Fox, took the lead and the race was a lock. Gallant Fox won it by four lengths. He became the eighth horse in American racing history to win $200,000. His Belmont victory gave him earnings of $203,730, to put him in a class with such as Zev, Display, Man o' War, Exterminator, Sarazen, Blue Larkspur, and Crusader. Today, money is confetti. You could beg for this much if you bum the right places. But in 1930 it was a big thing.

Woodward waited for the horse, then led him into the winner's circle like a guy bringing his wife out of church. Sande was as straight as an Indian in the saddle. Mr. Fitz walked alongside, then as Woodward and Sande went up to receive a trophy, Mr. Fitz turned and headed back to the barn with his horse. He had a smile on his face, but that didn't mean anything. It would have been there if he had lost.

By Monday, the newspapers were trying their best to make a big guy out of Mr. Fitz. George Daley in the *World* suggested Mr. Fitz be incorporated and listed on the big board. Nelson Dunstan in the *Morning Telegraph* said he was the greatest trainer of race horses the game ever had seen. He had taken a horse and had him hold his form through four major victories. Gallant Fox didn't give a hint of needing a freshener. The accolades became so widespread that it is quite possible Mr. Fitz might even have read one or two of them.

"You're a big man," Hype Igoe, the writer, said to him at Aqueduct on Monday morning.

"That's good," Mr. Fitz said. "What happens next week?"

"I don't know," Igoe said.

"Neither do I. That's why if you'll get the hell out of the way here I can go to work and protect my livin'."

From here on, the story seems to become something for a record book. Gallant Fox won the Dwyer Stakes, although Sande was horrified to find he had to hit his horse three times in the stretch to get him going. In Chicago, with $65,800 on the line for the American Classic, it was a bit different. Gallant Knight hooked onto him in the stretch and the Fox went to work on him. He was older by now and more experienced at the business of driving another horse crazy. He raced even with Gallant Knight, then 70 yards from the wire he got his head in front, his ears popped up, and he did everything but laugh at Gallant Knight. He lost one race that season—the 100–1 shot, Jim Dandy, beat him in the Travers at Saratoga. After that, Gallant Fox came back to beat Questionnaire in the Lawrence Realization at Belmont—with the ears popping up again, this time for a photographer.

At Belmont Park that day, there was a momentous occurrence. In the infield, up close to the far turn, was a crazy-quilt wooden house with several rods and smokestacks jutting from its roof. Inside, one Professor George Sykes, a gaunt, close-mouthed man, was stoking a furnace with stuff he was taking from a box. The fire sent up profuse clouds of black smoke. Standing away from the house, in a supervisory capacity, was a little man with gray hair parted in the middle, alert blue eyes, the carriage of a Prussian. He fingered a carnation in his lapel and smiled a bit as he watched the smoke rise into the soft fall air. This was James A. MacDonald, a magnificent man of forty-eight who introduced himself as Colonel John R. Stingo. He was connected with this smoke-making operation.

Its purpose was simple and tremendously important: the colonel and Dr. Sykes were getting $2500 from Joseph E. Widener to prevent it from raining.

Several days before, the colonel had been sitting on the shoe-shine stand alongside the betting ring at Belmont. He had only a couple of dollars in his pocket, but the ambition to hold much more than that. As he gazed over the mass of bettors and bookmakers, the Colonel saw a familiar figure. It was Dr. Sykes. Some years before, in Visalia, California, Dr. Sykes and the colonel had teamed up to take an amount of money estimated at $80,000 from farmers who sought relief from a bad drought which had hit the area. By shooting off an ancient cannon, doing it out of sight from the farmers, of course, they insisted they were making it rain. If the rainfall over a 32-day period was three inches or less they were to get nothing. But they were to be paid at the rate of $10,000 an inch if it came down to between three and four inches, more if it exceeded that amount.

The colonel, who believed simplicity was the key to any endeavor, whether honest or dishonest, had handicapped the deal. He had gone to the United States Weather Bureau, the Department of Agriculture, and other organizations devoted to helping a public which mostly does not know these aids exist. With long hours of study and figuring—"just as mighty a project as attempting to discover an overlay at Santa Anita," the colonel insists—he discovered the records gave him a tremendous edge for this period. The rainfall, over the years, was always three inches in that area. Chances were fine it would hit four. All the farmers knew was that they wanted rain. So on opening night, amidst much booming of the gun, a monsoon hit the area and one of the great swindles was brought off.

And now, at Belmont Park, here was Dr. Sykes. And he was talking to Mr. Widener, the president of the track. Talking rather quickly, with much animation and, judging by the nods of Widener's head, with much success.

"It was rather easy to see what was going on," Colonel

Stingo says. "This was the depression. Belmont Park, in its first full meeting during this national calamity, was finding it hard. Here with twelve days left in the fall meeting the crowds had fallen off because of the wretched weather and the lack of money in general. But if the weather were to shine favorably upon Mr. Widener's establishment, the track could at least break even on the meeting. Now suddenly we find Dr. Sykes on the scene. And doing well. It does not take a genius to discover the reason for this momentous meeting. Dr. Sykes was selling the sucker on a deal to make it stop raining.

"I departed from the shoe-shine stand in utmost haste and made my way to the gathering just as Widener was leaving. I took my dear old friend Sykes by the arm and inquired what was up. And in what way, if any, he could avail himself of my services. In other words, boy, I was taking a piece of his action.

"Lo! It was better than I suspected. The millionaires had actually brought him from California to protect their meeting against losses. He was a magnificent old fraud. He looked me right in the eye and maintained he could turn rain on and off as he pleased. Then he came down from the clouds just enough to make a little sense. He could use my meteorological research. He also could use a little help with money—tease, as I call it. And I'd have 45 per cent of the action.

"His deal was functional. He would put up $2000 as evidence of good faith. Then he was to stop the rain. For this, Widener was to pay $2500 on Saturday, $1000 on each weekday it didn't rain. In turn, Sykes was to pay $2000 on each day that the weather bureau reported even the slightest thing this side of a dew."

Sykes had informed Widener he used a special iodine-silver spray which would ride wave vibrations clear to the very heavens. They could change the climate of India with enough of their machines, they said. And in setting the terms, the $2000 show of faith was urgent. "Always give the fish at least a look at a blood worm," the colonel says. The colonel and

215

Sykes spent several evenings researching the weather for the area and noted that, as had happened in California, they had Nature going for them. Little rain occurred over the years in the twelve-day period they were about to handle. Then the colonel went out and got the $2000 from a Shylock, Sykes posted bond, the track advanced money to build his rain-prevention setup and the project which was to earn Colonel Stingo a name as "The Honest Rainmaker" was under way.

"I remember they had something out there," Mr. Fitz says. "It was Mr. Widener's idea. None of my business. I paid attention to the horse, not the people around, so I didn't know what they were doing. But I remember they had some sort of a house out there and they were doing somethin' in it."

"We were," the colonel recalls, "robbing another sucker, of course."

The colonel tells you this story in several places. At a bar in the Hotel Dixie on New York's 43rd Street. Or up on Eighth Avenue in a place called Gilhuly's, where he drinks profusely and, at age eighty or so, reminisces about the rain-making, or swings right into his present day interest. "We are specialists," he says softly, "in overlays. We do not advocate indiscriminate betting. When it is right, we are there. The public, a sucker as always, establishes a false favorite. Ours goes off at a magnificent price. The horse irrigates down the stretch and the boys who were on him fill their pockets with tease." He also told his tales at great length to *The New Yorker* magazine's Joe Liebling, and the material was later published in book form under the title of *"The Honest Rainmaker."*

At any rate, the day of the Lawrence Realization began with a dripping mist rolling in over Long Island from the Atlantic Ocean. Sykes kept disappearing into the house. The colonel stayed outside, ready to run at the drop of rain. By mid-morning the fog dissolved into fine sunlight, remained that way through the day and as Gallant Fox came on to nail Questionnaire and take it all for Mr. Fitz, Colonel Stingo had a winner for himself, too. It was a great triumph. "All that happened," he says, "is that it just didn't happen to rain on the poor boobs below."

For Mr. Fitz, the year 1930 was a big one. Horses he trained won $397,355, a tremendous sum for this time.

Gallant Fox was retired to stud at the end of that year. Two years later, when Mr. Fitz and Woodward were inspecting the crop of yearlings and weanlings at Belair, they were giving special attention to a couple of foals, including the first sired by Gallant Fox. The other was by Sir Gallahad III. Woodward by now had a great ambition. He wanted to have a winner of the English Derby and had been sorting out hopefuls from his stock and shipping them to England, where they were trained by Captain Cecil Boyd-Rochford. Woodward and Mr. Fitz thought the Sir Gallahad III colt was the best of the lot. The next year, when the horses were gangling yearlings, the colt still looked best. Captain Rochford was in the country to look at the stock and he and Mr. Fitz agreed on the colt.

"The Gallant Fox colt looks like he could be fine," Mr. Fitz said. "Take another look at him so we'll be sure."

They did. Both then decided on the other colt. Woodward had the horse shipped to England. The other, whom he named Omaha, was turned over to Mr. Fitz for racing. At two, Omaha was nothing to get excited about. He won only once in nine starts. But horses change from year to year and on the first Saturday in May of 1935 Mr. Fitz was standing in the paddock at Churchill Downs again and a blond-haired kid named Smokey Saunders came down from the jocks' room, swung up on Omaha and went out to the track for the Kentucky Derby. As the horses headed for the post, a slim, dark-haired newcomer, Eddie Arcaro, was trying to settle his first Derby mount, the filly Nellie Flagg, who was having the kind of trouble fillies usually have in the springtime. The track was mud, but it didn't bother Omaha. He was fifth at the half to something called Plate Eye, then he took over from Whiskolo at the three-quarter pole. At the head of the stretch, Saunders took one look straight ahead—"the finish looked so far away I nearly fell off"—then put his head down and didn't lift it until he was a winner. Roman Soldier was second. Two weeks later, in the Preakness, Firethorn ran second to Omaha and then in June, in the Belmont Stakes, Firethorn chased him again and got nothing. It was Mr. Fitz's second Triple Crown winner. You tend to dismiss a thing like this when you are dealing with him because he doesn't think it important at all. But only one other who ever lived, Ben A. Jones, trained more than one Triple Crown winner.

The colt they sent to England? "I forget his name. I know he didn't get anything, though."

In 1934, when he was having trouble with Omaha, then a two-year-old, Mr. Fitz had a barn full of horses who could run. One was Faireno, owned by Woodward, and the winner of the 1932 Belmont Stakes. The other was Dark Secret, owned by Mrs. Phipps and Ogden Mills. Dark Secret was the outstanding distance horse in the country in 1934, and won 19 races in his career.

On September 15, he took the track with Charley Kurtsinger on his back to run in the Jockey Club Gold Cup at Belmont, which is a two-mile race. There were only two other horses in the race. One was Inlander, which didn't seem to fit in, the other Faireno, whom Dark Secret had defeated in a race at Saratoga—the Saratoga Cup—a month earlier. The sky was black and a sheet of rain covered the track.

There was a crowd of 25,000. The big event had been the Futurity, won by Chance Sun. Omaha had finished fourth. Everybody was writing about that when the three horses came up to the starting gate for the Gold Cup. The gate opened and the horses began running. It was a match race from the start. Kurtsinger got Dark Secret out first, Tommy Malley had Faireno right on him. Inlander was out of it from the first strides. The two horses ran evenly around the huge, sweeping mile-and-a-half Belmont track, Dark Secret on the inside, Faireno, the outside. Mr. Fitz was in the grandstand, at the head of the stretch, watching his two horses run. Dark Secret and Faireno settled down into a duel of legs and lungs and hearts. These were two thoroughbreds out to do exactly what they had been born for, and there was to be no stopping. Dark Secret kept in front, now by a half-length, now by a length as Faireno held on. At the top of the stretch they started to pick up the pace. Malley's right arm began to go up and come down as he whacked Faireno. The horse lowered his belly, as race people say, and came on. Alongside him, Dark Secret picked up. His stride lengthened and came faster. This was one hell of a race and the crowd started to pick it up. The roar started way up the track, when the people in the grandstand saw the two begin their charge. Then it rolled through the stands and now the whole of Belmont Park was roaring. The two horses came down the stretch, with Faireno's nose now even with Dark Secret's flank. Both had come nearly two miles, but they were running straight, and harder every step. Kurtsinger had his face buried in Dark Secret's mane, his arms pumping forward with everything he had in his little body. He was trying to get home a winner and he was oblivious to anything else. But as they neared the wire Kurtsinger felt a lurch. Dark Secret had bowed a tendon in his right front leg. Dark Secret faltered. But only for a tiny piece of a second. So tiny only Mr. Fitz remembers seeing him do it. Then Dark Secret reached out with his injured right leg again and one thousand pounds of horse and Charley Kurtsinger's 118 pounds and the saddle and the lead pads all came down on the torn ligaments. He swayed. He kept going. He was a race horse, and he was racing. He was not going to stop until he was finished with what he was supposed to do. His feet slammed into the mud, his body strained, his head bucked up and down and he kept even with Faireno. He had the kind of pain you do not live with. But with yards to go Dark Secret kept charging while Faireno flew. He had to catch the crippled horse. But Dark Secret did not stop until he had his nose laid out so everybody could see he was the winner. Then he stopped. His right leg shattered directly under the finish line. Kurtsinger tumbled off, picked himself up and looked.

Belmont Park was silent. The rain beat down on Dark Secret's back as he hobbled in the mud. The rain dripped from his coat. But he was up. He was up straight, looking up the track. And his head was high, as high as a proud thoroughbred can hold it. He had won the race.

They got a van onto the track and a groom helped Dark Secret limp onto it. Then they took him to a barn where the veterinarian could look at him. When Mr. Fitz got there, Ogden Mills and Mrs. Phipps were standing with the veterinarian and the man was leaning over and looking at Dark Secret's leg. Grooms held the horse tightly so he wouldn't rear and kick out in pain. Then the vet straightened up.

"The leg is completely smashed."

"Can I do anything with him?" Mr. Fitz asked.

"He'd suffer too much," the vet said. "Gangrene would set in. You can't help him at all."

"All right," Mr. Fitz said. The others nodded, too. There was nothing to talk about. The horse had run himself to death.

The vet reached into his bag for a needle with which he would inject poison into Dark Secret's blood stream. It would kill him immediately. Mr. Fitz didn't even ask what it was. He asked the guy to wait for a minute. Then he started walking away. Mills called just a minute, to Mr. Fitz. He walked away, too.

"Me and him, we just walked away," Mr. Fitz says. "I wasn't going to look at that."

In the newspapers the next day, Dark Secret got a couple of paragraphs at the tail end of the stories about the Futurity, which was a very important race because there was a lot of money in it for the winner. Dark Secret's victory was only worth $6500 and that didn't make him very important at all.

In January 1935 the Wheatley Stable presented Mr. Fitz with a smallish two-year-old colt whose ancestry was Hard Tack-Swing On, so he had good folks, but that was about all. He was small and game, but couldn't run with the best. So Mr. Fitz began to make a hard worker out of this horse, who was called Seabiscuit. Mr. Fitz ran Seabiscuit 35 times as a two-year-old. The horse won four times against nondescript company. Then at Saratoga, on August 3, 1936, Mr. Fitz put jockey Jimmy Stout on him in an allowance race and Seabiscuit won by six lengths.

The next day, Mr. Fitz was sitting in a chair under a tree in the paddock at Saratoga when Ogden Mills walked over to talk to him.

"What do you think of Seabiscuit?" Mills asked.

"Nice little horse, but not real good," Mr. Fitz said. "I don't think he'll ever be much more than he is."

"Well, I have an offer from Charles S. Howard for the horse. He'd like to pay $7500 for him."

"Nice price for him," Mr. Fitz said.

Mills went away. Mr. Fitz heard nothing more of it. So he put Seabiscuit into a race on August 10. He won by four lengths this time. Later that day, he saw Mills walking toward the clubhouse.

"Say, if you're going to sell Seabiscuit," Mr. Fitz said, "you better get a little more than $7500 for him. The horse looks like he might start gettin' useful around here. Might pay some bills."

"No," Mills said, "I gave Mr. Howard my word he could have him for $7500 and I'm not going to change it now. The horse is his for that price. In fact, I'm going in to talk to him about it now."

The rest is in the racing books. Seabiscuit simply became a great horse. Any sports fan who is over thirty-one years old now will remember listening to Clem McCarthy's deep, thrilling voice coming over the radio as he called the great match race between Seabiscuit and War Admiral in November of

1938 at Pimlico race track. Seabiscuit, ridden by the late Georgie Woolf, the one they called the Iceman, won it by two lengths.

And in all the afternoons spent sitting with Mr. Fitz at a race track, and all the nights at his house, and in all the newspaper stories written of him, Seabiscuit is the only subject ever brought up that draws a hint, the slightest hint, that Mr. Fitz wants to say something to make himself look good.

"I raced him thirty-five times as a two-year-old," he was saying one particular night. "That's what brought the horse around. He never would have been anything if I hadn't run him thirty-five times as a two-year-old. You could put that down as something good I've done."

All through these years, day in and day out, whenever there was a big race, a Fitzsimmons-trained horse was shooting for it. In 1936, you had Granville, another Gallant Fox colt. He was almost as jumpy and unpredictable as a human being. They tried every trick in the book to calm Granville down. At Louisville, Mr. Fitz had his feed held out in the morning, then had him walked to the paddock as if he were going to run in the next race. The colt took it quietly. But on Derby day he began to fret and his sides turned to lather and when he got to the gate he jumped around like a school kid. At the start Jimmy Stout went sailing off Granville's back, landed on the seat of his pants and that was that. Two weeks later, in the Preakness, Stout was able to hang on, and got second money. By June, in the Belmont Stakes, Granville was rough. He slammed down the winner, then shipped out to Chicago and took the Arlington Classic. At Saratoga he won the Kenner, although he tried to fall asleep in the stretch, then took the Travers. On August 29 Granville ran a mile and three-quarters, for the Saratoga Cup, against the great Discovery. It was deep mud, but it didn't bother Granville. He won by six lengths and after it everybody was saying that the great Gallant Fox had outbred himself in this one.

Then in 1939 there was Johnstown, who could fly. He won

the Kentucky Derby, ran out of the money in the Preakness, then came back to win the Belmont Stakes. Big victories were five cents a pound for Mr. Fitz. The horses, every one of them, could have lost, he feels.

12. It Don't Hurt None

The little girl was about four and she came running into the barn ahead of her father. She wanted to look at horses, but she stopped when she saw Mr. Fitz. He was a strange sight to her. He was leaning on a stick which he had in his right hand and as it was mid-day by now, his head was heavier than it had been at 5:30 in the morning and he was looking directly at the dirt floor.

The little girl walked up to him, put her hands on her hips, and crouched down almost to the ground and looked up into Mr. Fitz's face.

"Poor old man," she said. "Look at the poor old man."

Then she turned and ran away to look at horses. Her father, who had come in a step too late to put a hand over her mouth, hung his head. He looked like he wanted to die.

Mr. Fitz kept looking at the ground. "Poor old man," he was saying. "Poor old man." Then he chuckled. He got a kick out of it.

There was also a morning when he was standing in the infield at Washington Park, Chicago, waiting for a man to tell him he could start talking to the two television cameras which were set up in front of him. He was going to explain what he was doing with Nashua, who was out on the track for a final workout before the big match race with Swaps.

One of the two cameramen stepped out from behind his camera and called to Mr. Fitz.

"Say," the cameraman said, "would you please pick up your head and look at the camera? I can't get your face the way you are."

Mr. Fitz's eyes brightened. "Son, if I can do that I'll give you Nashua," he said. Everybody laughed. Mr. Fitz loved the line. He made sure to remember to use it again.

This is how he has taken on the problem of having something wrong with his body that other people can see. Normally, this is a subject which can become deep and should be approached carefully. But this is preposterous when you are dealing with Mr. Fitz. For one thing, the physical trouble is totally unimportant as far as he is concerned. For another, he is a man who tells you what you want to know when you ask him something and he has little patience for delicate questioning, the kind where you get a person to talk about something without having to bring up the subject yourself.

One evening last winter in Miami, then, we were sitting with him on the porch of his house in Miami and we simply asked him what it was like to have little children come up and ask him why he doesn't stand up straight and to have adults, particularly if they do not know who he is, stare at him wherever he goes.

"Only one thing about it bothers me," he said softly. "You see how my head gets so far down? Well, I'm always afraid I'll be going along and I'll pass right by some nice fella and I won't even see him and say hello. He might think I'm givin' him the go-by. You know, sometimes when I got my head down I don't hear a fella say hello and I go right by him. He might think I'm kind of sluffin' him off. That bothers me a lot. I just wish I could see up enough so's I could say hello to all the people I'm passing."

He comes along on this kind of a road.

He expects everybody else to do it, too. In 1945, his grandson Jimmy, who had been taken apart a little by a shell in France, was brought in a wheelchair to Jamaica race track from an Army hospital where they were to spend two years trying to fix up his left leg.

Jimmy wanted to go over to see his grandfather, who was sitting in a car on the first turn, so he maneuvered out of the box seat they had him in, got out of the stands and then started over toward his grandfather. A guy from the race track, Larry Burke, came over to give him a hand. He pushed the wheelchair over alongside Mr. Fitz's car, then leaned in and spoke to Mr. Fitz.

"He's all right," Burke said. "Doesn't bother him at all. He's the same kid he was when he left here."

"Well, he wouldn't be a Fitzsimmons if he was around complainin'," Mr. Fitz said.

Physically, Mr. Fitz's trouble is that the vertebrae from the middle of his back to his neck have jammed together and ossified. This has taken all movement from his head. He cannot turn it from side to side. The best he can do is hold it up so he can see where he is going. This requires a lot of effort, so most of the time he looks down when he walks. When he goes to bed, his head is a full foot off the mattress because of the hump in his back. So Mr. Fitz puts an old lavender-colored jockeys' cap on his head, curls over on his side and sleeps like a bear.

Mr. Fitz, except for personal conjecture, never has been exactly sure of what his trouble stems from anyway and he has no idea what it will do to him in the future. This is because his relationship with doctors, except those doctors he talks horses with at race tracks, has been at best sketchy. In Miami last winter he had a supply of pills given to him by a doctor for some reason or another. The exact facts really don't matter because the pills, when last seen, were being taken by Ann Martin, his housekeeper. She figured they were for older people and since Mr. Fitz certainly wasn't going to bother with them she gave them a whirl. In recent years, Mr. Fitz has used two doctors, one in Florida and one in Ozone Park, but after handling the ills of race horses for seventy-six years he has a little bit of a notion that he can figure out humans, too, so he is not what you would call the perfect patient. He always put more stock in steam baths, light eating, no drinking or smoking and fresh air than in sessions with doctors.

"One thing the doctor down in Florida tells me," he was saying one night, "is the shape my heart and lungs are in. He says I'm as fresh as a fifty-year-old man. He figures the same way I do—I'm good for another twenty-five years."

Now, as for Mr. Fitz's old age problem. Apparently, this thing can be a whopper. A book written by a lady in Boston based on an old age center's study seems to indicate this. The book insisted that when a child reaches the age of four he does not, as we have always believed, simply stop biting people. Instead, he begins to establish a prejudice toward the aged. This gives you some idea of how tough it is to be old, because as everybody knows, it is really something to have four-year-olds hating you.

Mr. Fitz doesn't happen to be exactly in love with old people, either. As long as they revert to living in the past, he wants out. Late one Saturday afternoon back in 1957, he was sitting on a bench in the big waiting room at New York's Pennsylvania Station while they were making up the *Cincinnati Limited*. He was taking it to Louisville for Bold Ruler's shot at the Derby. For the trip, Mr. Fitz had on a dark blue suit, magnificent cowboy hat and a big bow tie. An old man in a black derby and string tie took the seat next to him, introduced himself and started to talk about the long, long ago. It seemed the most natural thing in the world for two old men to do, and Mr. Fitz looked like he was enjoying it. They were a wonderful study, these two old men sitting side by side, with the cowboy hat and the derby. But when a station agent came over and said it was time to get on the train, Mr. Fitz was muttering as he headed for the gate.

"Telling me all about Brooklyn seventy years ago or something," he was saying. "He thinks that's all I got on my mind. He's talking about seventy years ago in Brooklyn and I'm trying to win a race next week. Seventy years ago in Brooklyn. What good is that? I got no time for that nonsense."

In attempting to analyze Mr. Fitz's success at battling the years, all sorts of Bureau of Labor statistics are at hand to show that only a minute percentage of the population, 3.1 or so, is able to hold a job at eighty or over, and of this number only an infinitesimal few do much more than putter around at odd, part-time jobs.

Mr. Fitz's situation excited all the experts on the subject except Frederick H. Ecker, honorary chairman of the board of the huge Metropolitan Life Insurance Company.

"I don't see anything implausible about Mr. Fitzsimmons' case at all," Ecker said.

"How old are you, Mr. Ecker?"

"I'm ninety-three. You may reach me here at the office five days a week."

There have been many old people in the little part of the world called sports who were active to the last and, as far as the public was concerned, were as productive as ever. Only the slightest experience of being around these people, however, was enough to show that Mr. Fitz is one of the very few who consists of anything more than memories.

His age only makes him angry sometimes because he cannot do everything by himself any more.

"I got to rely on other people," he tells you, "and that's no good in my business. Now you take a thing like the inside of a horse's mouth. You've got to keep watchin' that all the time. Not just now and then, either. If he has a little cut or a sore in there, it'll bother him when there's a bit in there and he'll go against it. What you got to do is check the horse every day. Take aholt of his tongue and pull it to one side so's he won't bite you, then put your hand right in his mouth and feel all around. Make sure he's got nothin' botherin' him.

Well, I can't do that with every horse any more. And I tell somebody to do it and they wait and then they come and tell me, 'Oh, it's all right. I couldn't find nothin'.' Now I know they didn't do it right. But what am I going to do? Most of the time I just walk off mad. That's the only thing about bein' old that bothers me. I can't do them things by myself any more."

When it comes to matters pertaining to his personal finances, Mr. Fitz's mental ability is the same kind young Greeks bring with them to the shipping game. This was brought out the night we left his Chicot Court house so grandson Jimmy, who handles his legal and investment work, could go over some things with Mr. Fitz.

Later, Jimmy came around to Harry's bar and grill, picked us up and drove us home.

"He said, 'What have you got this over here for?'" Jimmy began. "'You told me last time it was supposed to be put down here. Now you got it over here. What for? You shouldn't be changing all these things. Keep 'em in order.'

"It was just one little thing. But that's what you are up against. Everytime."

Mr. Fitz also does not believe in taking it particularly easy on himself simply because of his age or back. You can find him, each night, riding one of those health club bicycles down in the cellar of his Chicot Court house. He grinds away for nearly a half hour, keeping a delivery boy's pace. Every few minutes he checks his watch to make sure he isn't doing too much.

"The heart," he says, "that's the thing I don't want to overwork. Nothing else matters. The legs? I should work 'em harder. There's nothin' the matter with them."

Mr. Fitz then, in everything, has the outlook of the lean toward life. And over the years he was not the only one in the Fitzsimmons household with this attitude. For he had, from the day he was married, somebody just as tough back home in the kitchen.

When Mr. Fitz was a mere seventy-two or so, for example, he stepped into the barn at Aqueduct to start the day and a dog named Apache rushed to greet him. Apache flew the length of the shedrow, slammed into Mr. Fitz's leg and bounced off. Mr. Fitz bounced, too. He went off the barn door and down to the ground in one motion. He broke his right leg as he fell and they picked him up and put him on the bed in the stable cottage. The doctor kept him there, the leg in a cast, for two weeks and anybody working for him wanted to beat the dog with a stick for causing this kind of trouble. Fitzsimmons stable workers now had the pleasure of taking orders from him for every minute of the day.

When Mr. Fitz finally was allowed to go home he decided to surprise his wife. He came into the front hall at Sheepshead Bay, dropped the crutches and began to pull himself up the steps backward. He would, he figured, get to the second-floor sitting room, then call for his wife. After much effort, he got up the stairs and entered the sitting room by hopping on one leg. He reached for a chair to balance himself. It was a fine new chair. It had been bought during his absence. The only trouble with it was it started to slide across the room when he put his weight on its arm. The chair kept sliding and Mr. Fitz, his bad leg held in midair, clutched the arm and started to fall forward. The chair stopped sliding only when it bashed into the wall and one of its legs snapped off.

The noise brought Mrs. James E. Fitzsimmons into her favorite room. She took one look at her husband, who was now stretched out, face down, on the floor, and let out a shriek: "Look what you've done to my chair."

Mr. Fitz, as the years went by and the family reached its sprawling size, became immovable on the idea that none of the younger generation in his family was going to attempt to make a living at the race track. And the years of winning had given him a hole card—he had money to pay the college tuitions. Anybody who wanted to work with horses was told he could try it if he went to college. That got the boy out of the way for four years and at the end of this period Mr. Fitz had a good argument: Why waste all that education on a race track?

His grandson, Eddie Carr, was talking about this one night. "I wanted to work out there," he was saying, "but the old man raised hell. 'Go to college,' he kept yelling. So I went to college. Then I still wanted to work there. So I had a little job taking care of some of the paper work for him, but he kept yelling about me wasting my education so much I had to leave and go and get a job. Look at Jimmy. He went to college to be an engineer. He still wanted to come out to the track. So my grandfather talked him into trying law. He went to school again and now he's a lawyer. The only one who's going to beat him is my kid brother, Bob. He's going to Cornell to be a veterinarian. In the summer he's supposed to take a job working around animals. Grandpop can't turn him down there. The kid was hot-walking horses this summer. Wait and see, he'll get the degree and sneak right onto the track and the old man won't have an argument against him."

Mr. Fitz thinks it is this side of a sin for anybody to follow him onto a track. "The big thing a kid should do is take care of his mind," he says. "Go to college. Then when you come out you see how much you don't know. So you can go and start learning what everything is about. But at least you've got the foundation for it. Now, after all that schooling, what sense does it make to get into a business of pure luck? That's all the race track is. Now I'm a winner at it. But I keep tellin' you, all them horses could've lost. What good is it to be smart if you're living depends on luck? If any of my kids want to get into racing, I'll let them. What they can do is go and get a job and make enough money to own a horse of their own. Then they can come out, hire a trainer and watch the horse run. Otherwise, no good."

Mr. Fitz, like anybody else who has made a living in a business where starving is casual, is against any moves but an old-lace-and-blue-chips kind of thing. His topcoat that became famous shows you that. One afternoon in the spring of 1950 he was wearing the garment around the barn at Aqueduct and it was simply too much for the late Harry King, a sportswriter.

"I'm with you, Mr. Fitz," King said. "But I'm not with that coat of yours."

The coat had a huge yellow streak across its back where sunlight, over many years, had bleached away the color. The collar was frayed like cheesecloth. The pockets and buttonholes were a mess.

"You must have taken a rooking on the coat," King said. "It didn't hold up at all."

"What's the matter with it?" Mr. Fitz said.

"It's all falling apart," King said.

"Show me where and I'll get it fixed," Mr. Fitz said.

With that, Sarah, who was in the kitchen, let out a moan. She had been taking that coat to a tailor near the track to have it mended from the first day she came to Mr. Fitz. The thing had become so embarrassing to her that she took to simply throwing the coat on the counter and leaving before the tailor was able to come out from the back and tell her, as he always did, "Maybe you should take one of my coats if he is having things so bad. I can't mend this. Here, take one of my old ones. Take. Take. Do anything. But don't give me this again."

This day, however, John Fitzsimmons saved her. "We're going to do something about this," he said. "We'll give the store a good dressing down for this."

Mr. Fitz kept looking at the fray marks and saying he was all for it.

The coat had been bought in a store called Hilton's, which once had been in Brooklyn but had moved to Broadway in Manhattan. John called the place, got the manager, and then complained eloquently about the way the coat had fallen apart. Mr. Fitz kept nodding in agreement.

233

"When did you buy the coat?" the manager asked.

"It was bought in Brooklyn," John said.

The guy from the store gave a big "What?" and then became excited.

"Please," he said, "forget the complaint. Tell me about the coat. We haven't had a store in Brooklyn since 1905. You still have a coat being worn which was bought in that store? Well, I'm going to put an ad in the newspapers about that."

The next day Hilton's window on Broadway was filled with pictures of Mr. Fitz standing at Aqueduct with his frayed topcoat which had lasted forty-five years. But Mr. Fitz would have been much more pleased if they had fixed up the coat instead of putting his picture in the window.

Mr. Fitz feels everybody should be like this. He gives plenty of advice on the subject and in one sad case, perhaps one of the most tragic in sports history, it was turned down.

That was in 1939 and the man he gave it to was Earl Sande. Earl stopped riding in 1934 and became a trainer. He was a success in that business just as he had been a success on a horse. In 1938, with Stagehand his top horse, Sande became the leading money winning trainer in the nation. With this kind of success behind him, Earl decided to go into the business of owning and breeding race horses himself. He did not think that there was a thing in the business of racing which he could not do with tremendous success.

But owning and breeding race horses is a proposition which a man shouldn't take on unless he has enough money to buy Russia. Short money, in this game, can mean a million. Which accounted for the summons Sande received at Belmont Park that summer. Mr. Fitz, who was in the paddock, wanted to talk to him. When Earl got there, the old man didn't waste words.

"Now look, Earl," he said, "I don't think you know what you're doing. Owning horses isn't for you. That's for big, rich guys. I don't care if you got a million dollars to your name. You need way more than that. Now you listen to me. You got the name. Everybody knows how good you are. You just sit back and let some rich fella get the horses for you and you train 'em. Don't you go around tryin' to own a lot of horses. It's too rich for you."

Sande listened quietly, smiled, and said thanks a lot to the man who had helped him so much. But as he walked away you could see he wasn't buying the talk. How could Earl Sande fail at anything?

It wasn't cockiness, either. At the time, it looked like the absolute truth. As a rider, Sande had everything, including to-the-bone honesty. As a trainer he won big ones. And even in his side line, singing, he was an unqualified success. He used to sing at private parties for his own pleasure, but when Sherman Billingsley first heard him he promptly booked Earl for his Stork Club. It was not a headline-getting affair, either. Sande had the warmth, smile, and Continental manners to project himself in a room like the Stork. And he had the voice. Some people sang in the shower. When Sande sang, he did it for big money in the Stork Club. That's how his life went and that's how he thought it would always go.

But it didn't. His breeding operation was based on hopes that Stagehand would become a great sire. He did not even come close. The horses Sande was trying to make it with were so bad that Frenchy Schwartz, the clocker, came over to him at Jamaica one morning and told him seriously, "Earl, you do better for yourself puttin' them things into cans for dog food. They gonna break you."

They did. The money went, the real estate went, the horses went, and in 1950 Sande wound up where he is today, living in one room on the second floor over a restaurant in Westbury, Long Island. Downstairs, in the big, immaculate taproom, a sheet of typewritten paper is framed. It begins, "Say have they turned back the pages . . ." It is the only reminder of who Sande is.

Sande has refused all kinds of help because his pride is that of one who has always won; won too much, perhaps, and

235

every time somebody offers him a job—many of them have
been for big money—he crumbles a bit inside. He thinks it
means charity. He says no. He wants to do it all by himself.
In 1953 he shocked the sports world by making a comeback
as a rider at age fifty-five. He had three mounts and on the
third, a thing called Honest Bread, he placed the horse well
and came down the stretch with just a little touch of the old
Sande in the saddle. And you could hear the cheer in the
stands. It was hard to believe that a racing crowd, whose only
hero is a winning ticket, would get excited over somebody,
but as Sande kicked Honest Bread down the stretch you
could hear the roar that race tracks heard all through the
'20s—"Come on, you Sande!" Earl won the race, but he was
dead tired and it was his last ride.

One night recently he talked quietly about the day Mr.
Fitz told him to stay away from it all.

"Money," he smiled, "I used to have a lot of money. Now I
don't have anything. I remember the day Mr. Fitz warned
me the thing would happen. Ah, but it was just another piece
of advice to me. I'd been advised all my life, and all my life
I'd done just as I'd pleased. I guess I should have listened to
him."

Sande is one of many stories in sports that causes you to
become disturbed inside when you run into them. The job of
handling money always is a problem for somebody in sports,
and particularly for somebody in racing. The money can come
in big and it can come in fast. And it is coming to a person
who many times is hit by the thing so hard that all he knows
how to do is turn the cash into confetti.

Mr. Fitz is not exactly in this pattern. In fact, you could say
that he treats a dollar as if it were a horse. And he has done
this for seventy-six years now. Nobody really knows what he
has in the way of money and it doesn't make much sense to
inquire because ten dollars or ten million dollars is not going
to make a human being like him. But mere browsing through
the record books show you that what he's made isn't hay.

His private business probably consists mostly of stocks and bonds, all of the kind that would hold up even in a depression. Most of his bets in the stock market were made for him by William Woodward, who understood that his client wanted to traffic only in things which were cement-solid.

Mr. Fitz's major business venture would have to be a thing called Bigeloil, a liniment. He purchased most of the stock of the company owning the formula and set up a small bottling plant in the '30s and has it running on about the same basis today. He also puts out a product called Fitzsimmons Leg Paint, which is usually applied to an ailing horse's leg, although expectant women, who flop around with leg cramps, can put it to excellent use. It does a fine job on the legs, although it can be hell on husbands because when you wake up in the morning you think you're rooming with Johnstown.

Bigeloil, according to the Fitzsimmons family, can cure anything this side of a coronary and they are not too certain but that it will prevent that. Mr. Fitz, each morning, sits down with a bottle of the stuff and plasters himself with it. He rubs his gums with it, gargles with it, paints his face and ears with it. His horses, similarly, are doused with quarts of the stuff after every workout.

Mr. Fitz's main business, however, is being himself and this is a unique business you are never going to find listed anywhere. You can't set a price on things like warmth and honesty. All the money ever made could not get for any man the reaction people always have when they first meet Mr. Fitz.

It is something which struck Catherine Drinker Bowen, the writer, one morning at Churchill Downs and she took note of it. She was at the track to see her first Kentucky Derby and early, while the horses were working out, she came to the dingy stable area and went over to meet Mr. Fitz, who was sitting in the early sunlight.

"You shake hands with him," she said later, "and you get a feeling that there is greatness in the man. How many happy mornings, you wonder, has he spent this way?"

An awful lot of them. Mornings can be the toughest part of life if you are having trouble with each day. For Mr. Fitz, who is old and bent over, the mornings are the best. They start another day for him.

CPSIA information can be obtained
at www.ICGtesting.com
Printed in the USA
LVOW04s2140230117
521932LV00013B/915/P